Finding DB Cooper
Chasing the Last Lead in America's only Unsolved Skyjacking

Martin Andrade Jr
With Martin Andrade Sr

Copyright 2016, Martin Andrade Jr.

All rights reserved. Cover photos are details from FBI flight path map, released by the FBI in 2010.

First Print Edition

Dedicated to Albert Reed McKay

Table of Contents

Introduction	9
The Heist	11
The Clues	17
Finding the Best Fit	23
Gunther and Cooper: Major Connections	31
Tena Bar Money Find	39
The Drop Zone	45
Problems with Gunther's Book	51
Math of the Tie	59
Surviving the Jump	63
Losing the Money	69
Cooper's Home	75
Why the FBI Failed	79
Finding Dan LeClair	81
Conclusions	85
Annotated Bibliography	91
Major Suspect Profiles	95
Minor Suspect Profiles	123
Larry Carr's Profile	129
Gunther Connections Annotated	135
Original Parachute Paper	141
FOIA Crew Debriefs	155
Original Crew Notes	189

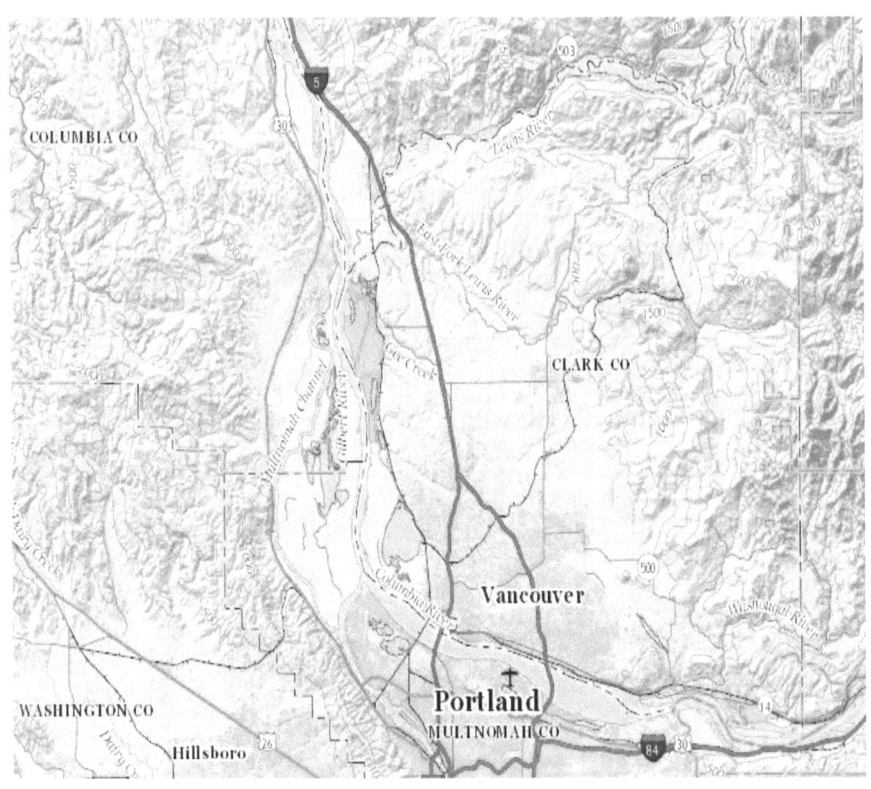

Map of Portland and Vancouver area, DB Cooper jumped somewhere between the north end of this map and Portland. Image from USGS.

Introduction

This book is the culmination of a two-year long investigation into the D.B. Cooper hijacking. I have long been interested in this case, but never had the time to study it in depth until a stint of unemployment gave me the opportunity. Originally, I was looking to write a novella about the skyjacking. While there have been a few attempts at fictionalizing the Cooper saga, I wanted to write one that was entirely based on the known facts, creating a realistic narrative about who Cooper was, why he hijacked Northwest Orient flight 305, and what happened to him after he made his leap from the back of the 727.

In the course of doing the research for the novella, I found out this case does not surrender answers willingly. There are strong disagreements among Cooper aficionados about nearly every aspect of this hijacking. Absolutely no agreement can be found about DB Cooper's criminal background, his skydiving experience, his race, educational background, his military experience, or whether he survived the jump.

Even worse, there is strong disagreement regarding parts of the case that seem to be well documented. The timing of Cooper's jump was originally calculated near Ariel, Washington and the FBI spent significant resources searching this area for any sign of the hijacker. Now it appears the FBI believes Cooper jumped farther south and somewhat to the east of their original search grid. The flight path of N467US from Seattle to Portland has also come into question. Surviving information is incomplete and later physical evidence suggests the aircraft might have been several miles east or west of the published estimate.

Even Cooper's appearance and general description have become topics of heavy debate. Originally, the flight crew thought he was in his 50's. Later, witnesses gave age estimates varying from late-thirties to as old as sixty. Cooper was described as having a dark complexion and being tall, around six-foot. Yet many people vociferously claim the eyewitnesses were mistaken.

Most of the real information in this case is argued over and discussed in several online forums devoted to this case. Norjack has a strong following among a small cadre of amatuer sleuths who endlessly discuss the excruciating details of the Tena Bar money find, the flight path, Cooper's identity and whether Cooper lived or died.

It's a fascinating ecosystem, but it's not for the faint of heart. The original Cooper forum was hosted on The Drop Zone, initialized as DZ, a website for skydiving enthusiasts. The thread was shut down after over 50,000 posts were published on the case. A few regulars from the DZ emigrated to the DB Cooper Forum (http://www.thedbcooperforum.com/index.php) where I joined the conversation a few months into my research. If you are truly interested in this case, I recommend joining us, at least for a little while.

Wading through all this material was quite a chore. Dozens of books have been written about this case, I read almost all of them. Few are really worth the effort but I wanted to be as complete as possible. Most are written to finger a specific suspect, which results in a great deal of confirmation bias. Typically, this has the effect of not only undermining the author's main thesis, but also discrediting much of the good research found in these books.

The turning point in my research was Tom Kaye's forensic examination of the tie DB Cooper left behind on the aircraft. Kaye's findings can be found on his website on the hijacking: www.citizensleuths.com. Kaye and his team found some exotic metals on the tie that would have been very rare in 1971. While I was still interested in writing a novella when I encountered Kaye, I made a change. In order to be thorough, I figured I should examine every suspect in the case to ensure none aligned with this new evidence. I expected to find nothing. I was wrong. There was a suspect in the case who would have been exposed to the exotic material Kaye found. We don't know who he really is or if he really existed (I do make the case for his existence later), but his story is outlined in the book by Max Gunther called "DB Cooper; What Really Happened".

This is when my interest in the case went from research for a novella to an actual investigation in search of a real person; the real DB Cooper. I have not yet found him, but I am very confident that he can be found given the right amount of time and resources. I outline how to find him later in the book. Besides making my case for what I call the "Gunther Hypothesis," I also looked at all the other major suspects that are publicly known. I believe each person can be definitively eliminated as Cooper. These suspect profiles are included in this book.

This book is primarily for those people already familiar with the Cooper hijacking. As such, I would direct those new to the case to read Bruce Smith's "DB Cooper and the FBI" and Ralph Himmelsbach's book "Norjak." Geoffrey Gray's "Skyjack" is another great book for those starting out. Finally, you won't fully appreciate everything I present unless you are familiar with Thomas Kaye's work on the case and after you've read Max Gunther's book. The hypothesis I hope to prove here is that Max Gunther's book tells at least part of the real story of DB Cooper.

The Heist

Giving a narrative of the DB Cooper hijacking is an obligatory part of any Cooper book. Since this is not a general book about the Cooper case, rather a very specific thesis, I will keep this very brief. Other books, especially Skyjack by Geoffrey Gray provide fantastic narratives about the actual hijacking. I would recommend the reader invest the time to get a proper appreciation for what happened on NWA 305 that day.

On November 24th, 1971, the day before Thanksgiving, a middle-aged man wearing a dark suit, carrying a briefcase, entered Portland International Airport sometime around 2pm. He purchased a one-way ticket to Seattle, paid in cash, with a twenty-dollar bill. He gave his name as "Dan Cooper" (this is how I will refer to him. "DB Cooper" is the legend; Dan Cooper is the actual man on the aircraft that day.) The plane was behind schedule, Cooper was observed in the waiting area standing alone.

When the plane finally arrived, Cooper was the penultimate passenger to board, sitting on the starboard side of the aircraft in row 18. Just before 3pm, the plane took off for the forty-five minute flight to Seattle. Just after takeoff, Cooper gives Stewardess Florence Schaffner a note, it reads "MISS – I have a bomb here and I would like you to sit by me" A few minutes later, Flo goes to the cockpit with the note while stewardess Tina Mucklow replaces Flo in the seat next to the hijacker.

Cooper's demands are simple. He wants $200,000 dollars and two sets of parachutes. He specifies two "front" chutes and two "back" chutes (this nomenclature is important as these are not skydiver terms). He sets a deadline for 5pm and orders the captain (Bill Scott, sometimes referred to as "Scotty") to keep the aircraft in the air until everything is ready to go. The passengers are not told about the hijacking; the Captain announces over the PA that they are burning off excess fuel due to a minor mechanical problem with the plane.

During this time, the cockpit crew is taking notes and communicating freely with air traffic control and their airline's flight operations. Tina Mucklow, the youngest and most inexperienced crew member, spends almost the entire flight with Cooper. She becomes Norjak's primary witness. She notes the kind of matches he uses to light his cigarettes. She observes that he can recognize Tacoma, Washington from the air. Cooper knows McChord Air Force Base is about twenty minutes driving time from the airport. Cooper is calm and polite, has no accent, and smokes Raleigh brand cigarettes. Cooper also displays a great deal of familiarity with aviation terminology.

On the ground, the FBI is already working on the case. The money is retrieved from SeaFirst Bank. The bills are part of a special fund set aside for these sorts of emergencies. Each of the twenties has already been photographed with all their serial numbers recorded. The money is bundled together with rubber bands and tossed into a canvas bank bag in such a way to give the appearance of being gathered in haste.

The parachutes prove more difficult to procure. We can't be certain exactly how this search was conducted It appears Cooper is first offered military chutes, but he refuses these out of hand. Eventually, two back chutes are borrowed from... *someone* and two reserve chutes, the "front chutes," are taken from a skydiving club in Issaquah. Unintentionally, one of the reserve chutes is a training device which, if used, would fail to properly deploy and kill the user. Cooper does not notice this mistake.

At 4:51pm, Northwest Airlines (NWA) President Donald Nyrup tells law enforcement to take no action. Cooper's demands are met and the flight crew cooperates with the hijacker. The plane lands at 5:43. At this point, most of the events are centered on getting the parachutes and the money onboard, offloading passengers, and refueling the plane.

Three fuel trucks were used to refuel the plane. Cooper apparently knew how long it would take to refuel the aircraft (twenty minutes or so), but this process took much longer than normal. The first fuel truck possibly had mechanical problems, the second truck ran out of fuel. It took a third truck to top off the aircraft. By the end of the ordeal, Cooper showed some anger and frustration with everything, reportedly saying "Get the plane on the road."

Tina Mucklow was allowed to exit the aircraft and retrieved the money and parachutes in several trips. Then passengers were released, and subsequently the other two flight attendants. Cooper kept Tina in the rear with him after the passengers exited. During this time, Cooper communicated with the cockpit, delivering his instructions on where to fly after the plane was refueled. He told them they were going to Mexico City, he wanted the airplane to maintain 10,000 feet with the landing gear and the flaps down. After some prompting from the crew, he asks for the flaps to be set at 15 degrees. This is important, since this was one of the indent flap settings on the 727, suggesting Cooper knew something about the aircraft itself.

Cooper was informed that, with a "dirty" aircraft, they couldn't make it non-stop to Mexico City. He was offered other locations, most of them along the Pacific Coast (Co-pilot Bill Rataczak wanted to drown him in the sea), to refuel. He refused all but the final option, which was Reno. Lastly, Cooper wanted the aft stairs (sometimes referred to as "airstairs" or "rear stairs") lowered during takeoff. The pilots would not allow this, and it was eventually agreed that the stairs would remain up during takeoff. Cooper told Tina he knew the stairs could be down for takeoff.

Just before takeoff, the crew was informed that a psychological profile suggested Cooper was going to force the stewardess to jump with the extra parachutes, and that Cooper would detonate the bomb and destroy the aircraft once he had made his jump. (Note: this is strong circumstantial evidence that the published flight path might be wrong, since the crew had before and after this made attempts to avoid populated areas. The believed flight path takes them over Portland. Forum member and Cooper Sleuth Robert "Robert99" Nicholson believes the aircraft went west to avoid Portland).

Sometime after 7:30pm, perhaps at 7:33pm, Flight 305 takes off from Seattle-Tacoma International Airport. At this point, it's understood that Tina Mucklow is explaining to Cooper how the aft stairs work. In a few short minutes, Cooper sends Mucklow forward. As she is closing the first class curtain, she notices he appears to be tying the bag of money to himself. This is the last time Cooper is ever seen.

Flight 305 had been cleared on Victor 23 down to Sacramento

before it would need to increase altitude and turn east for its approach into Reno. Cooper and the cockpit are communicating with each other throughout this time using the airplane's phone system.

[Over the course of the flight, several aircraft will be sent to monitor 305. Two F-106 Delta Darts, a C-130, a T-33 and a helicopter transporting FBI agent Ralph Himmelsbach. The two Darts could not fly slow enough to match the 727, so they circled around 305 in a large S-shaped pattern. The other chase aircraft were unable to intercept 305 around the time of the jump.]

At 7:40pm Cooper is struggling to get the aft stairs down. The co-pilot, Rataczak, levels the plane off at 7000 ft MSL and slows the plane to 160 KIAS (Knots-Indicated Air Speed). Two minutes later, the cockpit reports a warning light indicating the stairs were open. Cooper has released the stairs, but they don't go down like he probably expects. The airstream outside is actually keeping the stairs from falling into position.

At 7:45, the cockpit reports they are 19 nautical miles DME (Distance Measuring Equipment) out of Seattle and aren't communicating with Cooper. In all likelihood, Cooper is trying to figure out how to get the stairs to go down so he can exit the aircraft. He will eventually determine that he needs to put his own weight on the stairs to counteract the airstream from outside the aircraft. He figures this out sometime around 8pm. Weather is reported to the flight crew as foggy and hazy.

At 7:48pm, the crew reports they are ascending to 10,000 feet with flaps at 15 degrees. They reach altitude a few minutes later at 7:53pm and are flying between 170 and 180 KIAS. According to Rataczak, the flight was in icing conditions throughout the climb. Ice increases both drag and stall speed. As the crew increased airspeed to avoid a stall, they increased the air pressure holding the airstairs to the fuselage. Communicating to the cockpit, Cooper complains that the stairs won't come down. The crew, holding their breath, slows the plane.[1] Sometime around 8pm, a placard from inside the stairs' rear compartment falls to earth, to be found by a

---

[1] You don't know the stall speed in icing conditions like this, all you know is that it is higher than normal and you have little warning before the plane stalls. This was a big problem for Flight 305 because it is a dark night and they are flying over high terrain. ---MGAsr

hunter seven years later. At 8:01, Flight 305 reports they are flying at 160 KIAS.

At 8:05, after the flight crew had tried twice to contact the hijacker, Cooper comes over the PA and says "Everything is okay."

The hijacker is never heard from again.

Here's the real important bit: sometime around 8:11pm Cooper is on the stairs, preparing to jump or jumping. We're not sure exactly when Cooper jumped because the information hasn't been released. The other reason is there would not be a single "event" for the cockpit to report. Rather, there would be several key events. The act of walking on the stairs changes the flight configuration and requires the pilot to trim the aircraft. When Cooper jumps, the stairs would revert back to the original flight configuration, requiring the pilot to once again trim the aircraft. There would also be a pressure bump from the stairs slamming shut after Cooper jumps. While it appears the FBI knew when this pressure bump was, we don't know if it's at 8:11 or possibly as late as 8:16. One newspaper article[2] said these pressure events happened over a three minute period.

Regardless, Cooper is off the airplane before 8:20, when the time stamps reappear on the released flight transcripts and logs. During this time, the airplane is approaching Portland somewhere within the 8-mile wide Victor 23 flight path. Cooper is not seen jumping by any of the chase aircraft. He disappears from history. The only thing that is ever found from his jump is less than $6,000 of the ransom money that washes up on a sandbar in the Columbia River.

Flight 305 has an uneventful trip to Reno, landing safely at 11:02pm.

---

[2]From "Hijacker's Cash May Get Soggy" (UPI) on Nov 29, 1971 "'We've taken radar reports, it's all been computerized and we feel he's in this area,' [FBI Agent Tom Manning] said from his Woodland headquarters. The estimate was based on the plane's in-flight recorder, which showed when the hijacker lowered the 727's rear steps and a 'slight change in altitude' three minutes later, indicating he had jumped. "

The Clues

The Cooper Case has generated an endless crop of suspects; over a thousand individuals were investigated by the FBI at one point or another.[3] Now there are a dozen or so favorite suspects that are talked about on forums, in books and on the Cooper Wikipedia page. While there is some interesting circumstantial evidence for each of the suspects, no one has published what I believe is a definitive checklist of the clues and necessary characteristics to really pin down who Cooper was. Without a proper checklist, it's difficult to properly vet any of the suspects. So here is my checklist of Norjak clues and Cooper characteristics:

1) Comfort with a parachute and harness; Cooper put on his parachute with relative ease. He also refused a note given to him on how to use a parachute. When Tina Mucklow expressed concern that she might not be able to carry the parachutes aboard the aircraft, Cooper tells her the equipment is actually very light and that she'll be able to carry it without any problems. Any Cooper suspect needs to have a background that adequately explains why he was so comfortable with the parachute harness, and indeed comfortable with the very thought of jumping out of an aircraft at night.

2) "Negotiable Currency;" From the crew notes it appears that Cooper at one point asked for "negotiable" currency, which is an odd thing for most Americans to say. Only an international traveler, a foreigner, or possibly someone in finance would use such a phrase. Since Cooper spoke English without an accent, we can eliminate him being a foreigner unless he was from Canada. Particle evidence on the tie (discussed below) indicate Cooper likely didn't work in finance or banking, so we're looking for an American or

---

[3]This number exaggerates the investigation to appear more comprehensive than it might have been. In actuality, the vast majority of these "suspects" were convicted felons who were serving long sentences in state prisons. Federal prisons were considered more desirable, so false confessions were made by many inmates in an attempt to get moved from state to federal prisons. Its unknown exactly how many of these suspects this situation applied to.

Canadian who traveled extensively, including international travel. This severely limits the pool of suspects.

3) Knowledge of the Boeing 727; Cooper knew a lot about aviation and the 727 specifically. He knew the flap settings. He knew there was no locking mechanism on the doors (whereas other airliners had locks on their aft stairs). He knew the lingo, like what the phones on the plane were called. He was familiar enough with flying to know you could submit a flight plan after takeoff. That's simply too much knowledge to luck into or pick up from a book on aviation in the library.

4) Matches Physical Description; Cooper was definitely taller than one of the stewardesses. Probably around six feet. Middle age. He had a medium build, olive complexion and dark hair. Stewardess Tina Mucklow spent hours with Cooper, both when he was seated and standing. Stewardess Florence Schaffner was able to write down Cooper's description very soon after the hijacking started. Bill Mitchell, a college student seated directly across the aisle from Cooper, was attentive enough to notice Cooper and was jealous such a disheveled old man was getting so much attention from the stewardess.

5) Reminiscent of the Sketch; The FBI composite sketches are not perfect, but any Cooper candidate should be vaguely reminiscent of them. The sketches were based on descriptions from several people. While the details of the sketches changed a little over time, the general impression of Cooper having a high hairline, a sallow and emaciated appearance, and otherwise having an unremarkable face have been consistent in every iteration of the sketch.

6) Eyewitness Affirmation; There are still several living witnesses to the hijacking. Two of the stewardesses and at least one passenger had extended contact with Cooper. They should be able to give a thumbs up or down on any suspect. Later on in the book, we will meet some suspects whose pictures were almost assuredly shared with our eyewitnesses (and likely rejected). None of these witnesses speak openly about the case, so it will be impossible for amateur sleuths to get such affirmation.

7) Knowledge of Seattle-Tacoma area; While the plane was in the air, holding over Puget Sound, Cooper was able to recognize Tacoma and he also knew the travel time between McChord Air Force Base and the SeaTac airport. While it's possible Cooper could have gotten this information through intense planning and scouting, it's more likely he already knew the area. He probably lived or worked in the Pacific Northwest at some point in his life.

8) Whereabouts unknown during hijacking; Goes without saying, any Cooper suspect must have had an opportunity to commit the crime.

9) Smoker, preferably Raleigh Cigarettes; Cooper was at a minimum a casual smoker, a pack a day or so. He was probably not a chain smoker at the time of hijacking since he only smoked 8 cigarettes in about 8 hours. Particle evidence from the tie suggests he had been a smoker for a long time, and his fingers were stained with nicotine.

10) Dan Cooper Comics reader; This is entirely speculative. It would be nice to have some explanation for the origin of the Dan Cooper alias. Currently, the prevailing theory is Cooper had read the Franco-Belgian comic book series called "Dan Cooper." An American GI could have encountered the comic while serving overseas as early as 1957. The comics were written in French, so that would make Cooper bi-lingual (though he had no accent in English). This could all be a coincidence, and as such it is the least important item on the checklist since the "Dan Cooper" alias could come from anywhere. In fact, one of the anecdotes FBI agent Ralph Himmelsbach gives in his book "Norjack" is investigating a Cooper suspect, who was a jumper, who had supporting circumstantial evidence of involvement in the case, and whose real name was "Dan Cooper." Cooper could have gotten his alias from a phonebook. We don't know.

Evidence from the Tie

In addition to the above checklist based on the eyewitness accounts of the hijacking, there is new evidence recently found on the tie left by Cooper on the airplane (though there is a debate, like there's a debate about everything in this case, whether the tie is really his). I discuss the tie in detail in a later chapter, and I make what I believe is a strong case that the tie really did belong to Dan Cooper. However, there is a strong possibility of cross contamination with the tie evidence, especially when it comes to the DNA signatures found on the tie, so the evidence should not be taken without a little skepticism. (The analysis done on the tiewas conducted by Tom Kaye's "Citizen Sleuths" Cooper team.)

Clip-on tie user; The tie is a Towncraft #3 clip-on from J.C. Penney purchased between 1964 and early 1971 (this is based on research done by user "Farflung" the DZ forum). As a general rule, people are either clip-on tie users or not. While it is completely possible someone who wears regular ties would use a clip-on tie (perhaps as a safety measure for a parachute jump) for a skyjacking, I tend to think Cooper was a regular clip-on tie user. The density of particles on the tie also indicate it was worn frequently, and it was worn at his place of employment.

Pictures with similar tie clip; The tie clip found on the tie was a common design, sold for decades, so it is not a definitive test. However, the tie clip had been on the tie for a long time, in exactly the same spot, which would make photo-matching a suspect a possibility. A very good possibility, since Cooper put the tie clip in from the left side, not the right. This would make it possible to confirm the tie even from a fuzzy photograph. It may also indicate Cooper was left-handed.

Titanium Particles; Pure titanium particles were found on the tie, which would have been quite an unusual thing in 1971. Cooper could have only been exposed to this exotic metal at a few factories and chemical plants across the country. Other particles, including pieces of machined steel and aluminum, confirm Cooper worked in industrial chemicals. In 1971, there were four places in the US, including one in Pacific Northwest, where Cooper must have worked. Since we know when the tie was sold, Cooper worked in at least one these metal fabrication plants between 1964 and 1970. Since he wore a tie, he was likely a manager or an engineer.

Medication; Particles consistent with packing materials from prescription drugs were found on the tie, suggesting Cooper regularly took prescription medication for some condition leading up to the hijacking. We can't say for sure what he was taking, but blood pressure medications were the most commonly prescribed drugs then, and now.

Partial DNA Match; Some DNA was found on the tie. There are three distinct DNA sources, two weak and one strong. (The tie was most likely contaminated while being handled by numerous FBI agents after being collected in an era before DNA testing was available or even considered as a forensic tool). All of the DNA signatures are male. It should still be possible to get a match from a suspect to this DNA. This would definitely disprove any suspect, but it will not be able to confirm a suspect. Better DNA samples could have been collected from the cigarette butts Cooper left on the airplane, but that evidence was lost by the FBI. (This is a major loss, since the partial sample from the tie can't be compared to familial DNA. Also, a complete DNA sample could have confirmed Cooper's ethnic background and it's even possible to reconstruct someone's face from their DNA).

I have applied the above checklist to all the existing Cooper suspects, and from my results I found only two suspects that could conceivably be considered as having participated in Norjak. One is actually well-known to Cooper sleuths, and the other is the much-derided "Dan LeClair" from Max Gunther's book. I have included all my suspect profiles later in this book, however I don't explicitly examine every item from the above list in every suspect profile. Anyone interested in seeing my full checklist, with all the candidates, is welcome to visit martinandrade.wordpress.com and look under the "DB Cooper" tab.

Finding the Best Fit

When I first started looking into this case, it was my opinion that whoever DB Cooper was, he was not one of the suspects regularly talked about online or on TV. So I took the available evidence, read as much as I could, and created a rough overview of all the evidence. The end-product on this effort was the checklist seen in the previous chapter. I also wanted to form a coherent theory about who Cooper was and where he came from, and what might have happened to Cooper after he left the 727 with his parachute and bag of money. I outlined everything I thought happened, within a reasonable level of confidence. I have since attached myself to the Gunther suspect, but it is still a sound exercise to go through the evidence and create a best-fit narrative. I make major connections between Gunther's Dan LeClair and Dan Cooper later. (I posted an abbreviated version of this on the DB Cooper Forum.)

While the case is very complex, and many of the clues are subject to intense debate, and I have changed my mind about some of the theory presented below, this is my original thesis from on in my investigation, before I was aware of Max Gunther's book.

Who was Dan Cooper?

First and foremost, Cooper was not a criminal before hijacking the airplane. The FBI has, at the very least, some partial fingerprints from Cooper. They had years to investigate suspects with a documented criminal history. They did look into suspects with a criminal background, hundreds of them. If Cooper had been a known criminal, the FBI would have found him. So, when Himmelsbach says Cooper was "an old con," he's making a fundamental error. In all probability, the hijacking was Cooper's first crime.

From Tom Kaye's analysis of the tie, we get a fascinating picture of Dan Cooper. He was educated, worked as an engineer or manager. He could have been a metallurgist. Cooper possibly worked at Boeing on the 727, which would explain some of his knowledge of the airplane's rear stairs and flap settings. The timing of the hijacking is also of interest, as it took place just after the supersonic transport (SST) program lost its federal funding. Lots of SST workers lost their jobs.

Since the tie did not have any wild pollen on it, we don't know where exactly Cooper lived. The FBI took a long look at Boeing and its employees during its investigation, so Cooper was not a current or recently released employee there. Parts of the SST program were being worked on all over the country, so we again can't pinpoint Cooper's hometown. We do know, based on the knowledge he displayed during the hijacking, that Cooper lived in the SeaTac area at some point in his life, probably before leaving Boeing and pursuing a job in aviation at some other company.[4]

Cooper was ex-military. He was either a paratrooper or a loadmaster. He was literate, well-spoken, and level-headed. He was a casual smoker and a light drinker. He was taking some form of prescription medication, probably for heart disease. Since he asked for "negotiable currency" and his name "Dan Cooper" might have come from a French-language comic book hero, Cooper could have been born and raised French-Canadian before emigrating to the United States. Cooper was either a lifelong bachelor or recently divorced; he made his jump the day before Thanksgiving, so it's unlikely he was worried about needing to be somewhere during the holiday. He need not have been a loner, as Cooper remained quite calm and conversed for hours with a complete stranger, showing a high degree of social skill.

Much has been made of Cooper's "olive" skin tone. It could mean he was of Hispanic descent, though many Frenchmen have the same dark complexion and dark hair. He may even have been an avid outdoorsmen or golfer. Hang around a golf course in late August and early September, plenty of guys sport a deep tan. I mention golf because it's a universal business sport, and Cooper was probably a white collar worker.

---

[4] We now know, thanks to Kaye's analysis, that Cooper most likely worked at one of 6 Industrial Chemical facilities in the world between 1964 and 1970.

Making the Jump

Cooper probably survived the fall from the aircraft. I base this on several months reviewing hundreds of combat jumps made by RAF airmen during nighttime missions in WWII. From my study, I believe there exists a solid data set to make some reasonable inferences about what happened to Cooper between the 727 and the ground, and that inference is that he pulled the ripcord on the parachute and survived.

I go into more detail in the chapter on the jump, but here's my key finding: During WWII, if an airman was able to get out of his stricken aircraft in a conscious state and with enough altitude to deploy his parachute, there was an almost 100% pull rate. In fact, I couldn't find a single confirmed example of a no-pull casualty in the sample I had.

Some of the interesting jumps these airmen survived include: an RAF airmen who had to attach his parachute in freefall, in the dark; another who had a 20mm cannon round sticking out of his thigh; a successful jump with a parachute clipped to a harness on only one d-ring; dozens of guys thrown from exploding airplanes who managed to pull their ripcords; and more than a few who lost consciousness during their free fall and still woke up in time to pull their ripcords, deploying their parachutes. These examples are important because these airmen were inexperienced jumpers with little to no training. That they always seemed to find a way to activate their parachutes is indicative of the human will to survive even in such an odd situation such as freefall.

It's safe to say that, at some point during the freefall, Cooper pulled the ripcord. It would have been a hard opening.[5] He might have lost his shoes as he canopy unfurled, as he was reported to be wearing slip-on loafers. I believe he also lost the bag of money at this point. During the hijacking, Tina Mucklow saw Cooper trying to tie up the money bag with paracord. If you've ever worked with it, you'll know that paracord is difficult to tie into strong knots.[6]

---

[5] Freefalling from a high altitude, probably not in a stable, high drag position, Cooper would have been falling faster than 130mph. ---MGAsr

[6] Paracord is easier to tie in knots than you would think, as long as you have a source of fire, like a lighter, to melt the frayed ends.---MGAsr

The amount of force involved in a parachute opening is not very kind to improvised fasteners. At least one of Cooper's copycats lost their money during the jump.

Because Cooper was likely not a skydiver, he probably pulled the ripcord early, likely as soon as he stabilized into freefall. Remember, it was dark, and Cooper had no way to judge altitude. This means Cooper would have been pushed by the wind for a very long time and might have traveled up to seven miles, but probably more like 4 miles, to the east-northeast of his jump location. If the published FBI flight path is accurate, he landed a few miles east of Battleground, WA (figuring out where Cooper landed is discussed in a later chapter). This was mostly farming country, and pretty flat.

It would have been a blind landing; there was no moonlight. It would not have been totally dark, as there would have been some light from Vancouver and its suburbs. Still, there would not have been enough light for Cooper to be really prepared for impact.[7] There would have been a fifteen mile-per-hour wind.[8] If you want an idea what this landing would have been like, try jumping from the top of a car moving 15 mph with your eyes closed and no shoes. It would hurt. Paratroopers are taught how to land in ways that minimize injury, but this would still be a tough landing. There's a very good chance he was injured, a broken ankle or a fractured spine. Or worse. Somewhere around half of RAF airmen I looked at were injured in their jumps (airmen were not trained paratroopers, so this isn't surprising), but almost all of them were mobile and had the ability to evade capture for a little while after landing. Thus, Cooper was probably capable of moving away from his landing zone. In the dark, with at least ten hours before an air search would be able to find him, Cooper would have plenty of time to make his way out of the landing zone.

The Escape

Landing in a field somewhere, Cooper would move quickly to

---

[7]Paratroopers are trained how to land safely at night, the danger of injury would have been if he hit a rock or uneven ground.---MGAsr

[8]In the U.S. Military, parachute operations during training are cancelled if the wind is more than 13 knots (about 15mph). ---MGAsr

either a road or shelter. He probably buried his gear or just tossed it into deep brush. It's possible he was able to get a ride from someone, likely telling a story about a car accident or something. Since the FBI checked all the hotels and motels right after the hijacking, Cooper probably either stayed with his helpers for the night, or was able to get transportation out of the area.

What about the manhunt? What about the roadblocks? Cooper likely landed farther south than the FBI thought. The actual manhunt was undermanned and was in the wrong area. If Cooper was able to go south into Vancouver, WA, or hitch a ride east, there were no roadblocks to worry about. If Cooper was living in Portland area, it's completely possible he got a ride all the way home that night.

Cooper had paid for his plane ticket with a fresh $20 bill, and later used another $20 to pay for a drink on the airplane, getting eighteen or nineteen dollars in change. So he had some money on him other than the ransom money. If I were planning this caper, I would have plenty of cash on me. Even if Cooper lost the ransom money, he was not without resources.

If anyone did help Cooper and later came to be suspicious of the shoe-less and injured man they drove to Portland, they might have been afraid to talk about it, lest they be arrested as accomplices. Chances are, Cooper's story stuck and they never even considered the stranger they met 12 miles south of the FBI search zone to be anything other than the world's unluckiest dude.

The Money:

Three bundles of money were found on a sandbar about twenty miles away from the drop zone, and there's no reasonable way to explain how the money traveled so far with rubber bands still attached. The find was also upstream from the watershed where the the FBI believed Cooper landed in. The general conclusion I draw from everything I've read about the Tena Bar money find is that it is indecipherable. No explanation presented comes close to explaining the details of how the money got there.

If Cooper lost the money in the jump, like I suggest above, then someone else must have found the money. Greed would keep the find a secret. While there were rewards for helping to apprehend Cooper, they did not add up to the $200,000 in the bag. Even after the statute of limitations had expired, the people who found the money would still owe taxes on their windfall. Not too shocking, then, that these people never talked.

The FBI revealed a couple of years after the hijacking that all the serial numbers on the bills had been recorded, and they suggested that the money was therefore unspendable. If someone had found the money and was given the impression they would go to jail (or owe a ton of money to the IRS) if caught with it, I'm sure they would have disposed of it. Like by throwing it into a river. Or maybe they buried it near the Columbia. Some of the Cooper forum members have suggested the money looks like it was burned. It's possible someone tried to completely destroy the bills by throwing them in a fire, not noticing the several bundles that weren't completely incinerated.

These are all just guesses, and details surrounding the Tena Bar find are among the most speculative to be found in this case. Regardless, Cooper lost some or all of the money, and some of it ended up at Tena Bar. Anyone who might have found the money would have little incentive to talk about it, and we're all waiting on some deathbed confessions to move the case along in this area.

The Rest of the Story

Cooper, injured and broke, probably watched the news non-stop for the next couple of weeks. After making his escape, he might have taken all his available resources and left the area for good. Or, he could have stayed and returned to his regular life. He did his crime the day before Thanksgiving, a four day weekend, so his coworkers would have assumed he was with family. He comes in on Monday with a new tie, new shoes, and maybe a limp from a "car accident."

He makes no large purchases. His lifestyle doesn't change. There's no way to connect him to the crime. For whatever reason, the artist sketch doesn't quite look like him (much like the Unabomber case) and there's simply no one who can put him on that airplane. Besides, Dan Cooper was a white collar guy, a regular

Joe Doakes, he was boring. No one would believe the metallurgist on the shop floor was jumping out of airplanes. Above all, Cooper doesn't talk to anyone. Ever.

Long suffering from a chronic medical condition, Cooper dies sometime before Unsolved Mysteries airs its DB Cooper episode (October, 1988), the one with the new and improved artist sketch. Some of his co-workers mourn his passing, maybe he had a few close friends. A nephew shows up to his funeral. His ex-wife skips the whole affair. It turns out to be the greatest adventure never told.

There you have it, my original theory. As I present the case for Gunther's suspect, I will reference parts of this narrative. However, other parts are no longer completely valid. For one thing, Cooper probably never worked for Boeing, since we know this was investigated thoroughly by the FBI. He probably did not work on the 727 either, since that is a different industry than industrial chemicals. I also no longer believe Cooper landed near Battleground, WA. I put him somewhere in Vancouver's outskirts. But I'm getting ahead of myself. We'll take a closer look at Gunther's suspect in the next chapter.

Gunther and DB Cooper: Major Connections

Let's get down to business. Who is this suspect from Mr. Gunther? Who is "Dan LeClair"? Well... Dan LeCLair is the pseudonym for an anonymous Cooper suspect presented in a book by a long-deceased author about a much-lampooned love story involving a lonely divorcee and D.B. Cooper. For decades, this book was maligned by all those in the Cooper world, generally dismissed out of hand by serious researchers.

The book was written by Max Gunther, who was best known as a financial writer (his best seller was "The Zurich Axioms"). In 1986 he wrote "D.B. Cooper: What Really Happened", in it he describes being contacted by someone claiming to be D.B. Cooper shortly after the hijacking. Gunther received a letter or letters from this person, who hoped Gunther would "write his story." Eventually, Gunther even talked to this person on the phone[9] This individual later flaked, and Gunther forgot about the whole affair for more than a decade.

In the early 1980's, he was contacted by a woman through the mail. She was known to him only as "Clara." She claimed to know the real Dan Cooper, saying the mysterious hijacker had recently passed away. After a few letter exchanges, Gunther interviewed the woman six times over the phone for about an hour a session. Then, she too, flaked. Gunther was able to put together the story into the form of a book, researching and doing interviews with case principals to fill in the gaps, and it was immediately considered a hoax by the FBI. The book was forgotten about except among a few diehard Cooper aficionados.

Gunther's story got some revival when a woman named Jo Weber read the book and it somehow convinced her that her former husband, Duane Weber, was Dan Cooper. Over the course of a decade or so, on the original DB Cooper thread on the DropZone website, Jo presented her case and was excoriated for

---

[9]Like in a spy novel, Gunther was sent to a public phone in a busy building in New York. He described the caller as "articulate, unremarkable and unaccented." (Gunther, p 6).

her ambiguous statements and shifting positions. And rightly so. But along with attacking Weber, the forum members also tore down the Gunther book, almost solely by association.

The end result is, to my knowledge, no one has fully investigated Gunther's suspect.[10] So, at least in this chapter, I will quickly present the reasons why I think "Dan LeClair" deserves a closer look. Of most interest are those items that match recent revelations about the case that didn't become public, or weren't even discovered, until long after the book was published[11]

Cooper left his clip-on tie behind on the 727, on the very row of seats he had been sitting on throughout the hijacking. This tie almost certainly belonged to Cooper, as the likelihood of someone else leaving a tie on the plane under the given circumstances are negligible (Kaye, 2010). The tie had numerous metallic particles on it, including bismuth, unalloyed titanium, steel and other metals used in industrial processes. In 1971, unalloyed titanium in particular was rare, and was only found in a few places, including aviation research and industrial chemicals (Kaye). In general, only managers and engineers would regularly wear ties in these industries, limiting the potential population of Cooper suspects to a very small pool of people. Here Kaye describes his findings:

Titanium was a rare metal in 1971 and this makes it extremely unlikely it is a post-event contamination. Its presence constrains Cooper to a limited number of managers or engineers in the titanium field that would wear ties to work. This is also consistent with his mannerisms during the hijacking where the flight attendants described him as an "executive" [6]. The fact that he was also comfortable enough to pull off the hijacking wearing a suit suggests that it was a regular part of his wardrobe, again consistent with a manager or engineer type. Given pure titanium with embedded stainless steel, spiral chips made from

---

[10]The FBI has not released their files on the case, so we don't know how fully they looked into Gunther's claim

[11]I have asserted my belief that Max Gunther's book "DB Cooper; What Really Happened" tells the story, at least part of the story, of the real Dan Cooper. Most other Cooper researchers disagree, citing the numerous errors and problems in the text itself. I will answer those objections in a later chapter. My purpose here is to show the strong connections between details given in the book, and what we now know about the Cooper Hijacking. I will primarily focus on the evidence unearthed by Tom Kaye and his team, and will occasionally cite other sources, including documents that have come to light in recent years through FOIA requests and other public releases.

aluminum and other exotic metals, gives a "best fit" indication that Cooper came from or regularly visited a metal fabrication facility. These types of materials are known specifically for their corrosion resistance and commonly used in highly corrosive environments, such as chemical factories. A suspect having worked in a machine shop or a company that used pure titanium in a corrosive processes would be a good match to the family of particles found on Cooper's tie.

Max Gunther's Cooper Candidate worked in one of the industries where someone had a chance to be exposed to unalloyed titanium and the other particles he found. This is the primary link between the book and later evidence.

The odds Gunther made up the fact about Cooper being a salesman, manager or executive in the industrial chemical industry is very low. Perhaps thousands to one. A fuller analysis is detailed in another chapter where we can get a good approximation for how unlikely this event is. My calculations put the number at nearly 2,000 to 1.

In Gunther's book, Dan LeClair leaves behind his miserable job and unhappy marriage to set out on his own a year or two (or more, we can't be certain) before the hijacking (it has to be after 1964 based on the tie, which was sold between 1964 and 1970). The way he decides to disappear is key. He tells his wife that he's going on a business trip, gets dressed in his normal work clothes, and leaves. He arrives at work, tells everyone he's feeling very sick, and tells them he's going home. The he disappears… wearing his everyday work suit, with its collection of titanium and other metal particles.[12]

Working back through the text, we can find still more connections, some of them strong, some extremely circumstantial. I will try, throughout the book, to differentiate Dan Cooper the hijacker from Dan LeClair the suspect, even though I think they are the same person. Both their first names are "Dan" so I'll mostly

---

[12]Gunther describes a previous attempt by LeClair to disappear by faking his own death while on vacation, swimming in the ocean. It would have made for a better story, but it also would have resulted in LeClair leaving his work clothes safely tucked away in the closet at home. The 'faked death' narrative is a better story than the later explanation, making the idea Gunther invented everything to sell a book and make some money much less believable

label them with their last names.

– LeClair wore glasses, something he needed since his senior year of college. Immediately after absconding, he would remove the glasses to change his appearance (though he stopped doing this after a short period of time.) In the FOIA Interview briefs[13] stewardess Alice Hancock stated she believed the sunglasses Cooper was wearing were prescription, or at least looked like prescription sunglasses.

– After the hijacking, once he had established a relationship with Clara, LeClair purchased a bottle of brandy for the two of them. He used his own money for the purchase but none of the bills he used were twenties. We know Cooper used a twenty dollar bill during the flight to purchase a drink (before he hijacked the aircraft) and received about nineteen dollars in change.

– Cooper used a homemade bomb, and some of the particles found on his tie were tooled and otherwise manipulated by machinery. LeClair was described as being a handyman, with high mechanical aptitude and a preference for hands-on work.

---

[13]These FOIA documents appeared mysteriously a few years ago, copies are available on the DB Cooper Forum website (http://website.thedbcooperforum.com/). Transcripts of the documents are included in the Additional Materials section of the book.

– Cooper was described as an "executive type" by one of the stewardesses (this description is also found in the FOIA crew interview/debrief documents recently released on the DB Cooper Forum) and was conversational, pleasant and polite to everyone during Norjack, expressing anger only during the refueling process. LeClair had a similarly pleasant personality. It was so disarming that Clara "lost all fear" of the strange man sleeping in her tool shed after only a few minutes of talking to him.[14] LeClair also worked as an executive, both before and after the hijacking.

– "Dan Cooper" was a Franco-Belgian action-adventure comic book available only in French. LeClair was French-Canadian and an avid reader of "True" magazine, a male-oriented rag filled with action-adventure stories. It's never explicitly stated LeClair read comic books, but "True" magazine published stories very similar to those found in the Dan Cooper comic series. If LeClair traveled to Canada to visit relatives, he likely would have encountered this comic while looking for a copy of True Magazine.

– FBI agent and former Norjak Case Agent Larry Carr produced a detailed profile of DB Cooper and released it on the DropZone Cooper forum (Carr's entire profile is included later on in the book). The profile says Cooper had "just enough knowledge to be dangerous" and was a "smart aleck". LeClair was college educated, but not described as an academic, preferring hands-on work. He was not an intellectual, as he read men's adventure magazines, and his letter to Gunther is literate but Cooper "had not shone in English composition" to quote Gunther.

– Only one witness is reported to have seen Cooper's eyes, which were described as "brown," LeClair is described with "dark brown, almost black" eyes.

– Cooper was knowledgeable about the 727 and aviation in general. According to Gunther, LeClair was a regular flier before leaving his

---

[14] Bismuth particles found on the tie were associated with glitter makeup, making Cooper a possible "ladies man." This matches the description of his high degree of social ability and adds an interesting wrinkle to Dan LeClair's marriage problems.

family. In fact, he avoided traveling by air after he left for fear of being recognized. While planning the heist, LeClair researched the 727 using an unrevealed airplane reference book, and also through a pilot friend.[15]

— Gunther hints several times of LeClair suffering from chest pains. Faking chest pains was part of his original plan to fake his own death. After the hijacking, LeClair is warned to manage stress because of high blood pressure. Finally, LeClair dies in his late 50's or early 60's of a heart attack. Among the other particles on the tie, evidence of prescription drug use were found by Kaye.

-Gunther implies LeClair spent some time doing stakeouts at Portland airport. Cooper had at least two "Skychef" matchbooks with him during the hijacking. Skychef was a restaurant and food service chain that catered specifically to the aviation industry, and they had a restaurant in the Portland Airport, which they advertised in the local Portland papers.

— According to the book, LeClair avoided drinking and eating so he wouldn't have to take any bathroom breaks. Other than the first drink at the beginning of the flight (of which Cooper later spilled about half), Cooper refused all refreshments and snacks offered by the stewardesses during the ordeal. (If true, LeClair wasn't entirely successful, he slipped into the bathroom for a few minutes while on the ground in SeaTac when Tina Mucklow was away getting his parachutes and money.)[16]

— In the book, LeClair has to find a suit jacket and pants to go along with his plan, and he needs to be able to wear a skydiver's jumpsuit underneath it. Being generally poor, LeClair can't afford a

---

[15]It's doubtful any reference guides would help, several were looked at for this book. Mark Metzler was a skydiver who collected Boeing airplane manuals, and according to him those manuals said nothing about the 727 being able to fly with the aft stairs deployed. Actually talking with a 727 pilot might have been helpful to understand some of the problems a hijacker would face jumping a jet, but not whether the 727 could be jumped. In fact, LeClair asked his 727 pilot friend directly whether someone could skydive from the aircraft and was told unequivocally "no."

[16]Some researchers believe Cooper spent more than a few minutes in the rear lavatory while the plane was on the ground to deter snipers.

new one. It's unknown exactly what LeClair does, but Clara sees LeClair wearing pants that fit "baggily" when she finds him. Norjack eyewitness Bill Mitchell says Cooper dressed unfashionably, in ill-fitting clothing that did not color-match.

Other than the connection between the titanium particles and LeClair's work history, no single element explained above is definitive. Taken altogether, however, there's a strong association between Dan LeClair and Dan Cooper. The evidence from the tie creates the only physical link between any suspect and DB Cooper.[17] Kaye's findings says Cooper was a manager or engineer in the industrial chemical field. Thus we can make a very strong case that Clara was a real person who told her story to Max Gunther to the best of her recollection, and that she knew the real Dan Cooper.

---

[17]Sheridan Peterson is a candidate who might have been exposed to unalloyed titanium while he worked at Boeing, but it would not have been one of his primary jobs duties. His profile is included later.

The Tena Bar Find

According to Gunther, Cooper lost nearly half of the ransom money in the jump. My theory as to exactly how this is possible based on Gunther's text will be dealt with in a later chapter. My goal here is to give a general overview of the Tena Bar[18] find and the current theories regarding how the money got from the original FBI search area to a popular fishing spot on the Columbia River some twenty miles away.

In 1980, the story goes that a young Brian Ingram went digging in the sand on Tena Bar just off the Columbia River, just downstream from Portland and Vancouver. We're not sure how he found it. Maybe he was helping move sand to help build a fire pit. I tend to think he was just an eight-year-old kid playing in the sand. Regardless, Brian found a compacted chunk of soggy something. This something turned out to be about three bundles of the original ransom money, with the rubber bands used by the bank still attached. The family took it home and tried to separate the bills, using soap and even bleach, but weren't able to do much with it. Some of the bills dissolved during this process. They later learned about the Cooper hijacking and the ransom money, and contacted the authorities. The FBI took possession of the money and later searched Tena Bar for more clues, finding nothing but an indeterminate number of bill fragments.

It has to be remembered how unbelievably unlikely it was that this money was found at all. These three bundles had been in "the wild" for eight years. While in all likelihood the money was protected from the elements by the bank bag or by sand for most of this time, it was still outside of human control. The fact some of the bills literally dissolved when the Ingrams found it is a key indicator the money was near the end of its "findable" state. Given these circumstances, having a money find to talk about at all is a

---

[18]There is some controversy whether it should be called "Tena" or "Tina" bar. The sign at the actual site says "Tina Bar" whereas historical research says it was originally "Tena Bar." Since the primary witness in this case is Tina Mucklow, some people make the connection between the two. In fact, I originally made a connection between the two. To avoid confusion and conspiracy, I go with the original name for the site here.

miracle in itself.

Unfortunately, for our purposes in trying to analyze this discovery, this means the money was not found under controlled conditions. The Ingrams washed and dried and otherwise manipulated the money before it could be studied scientifically. When the FBI did their own recovery operation on Tena Bar, it included a bunch of agents haphazardly shoveling into the sand, further contaminating the scene. A scientist, geologist Leonard Palmer, wasn't brought in until the second day of the FBI operation. Worse for amatuer Cooper slueths, while pictures and reports of the FBI dig are with the Norjack case files, they are not available to the public. All of the analysis done by Cooper aficionados has been done with limited access to these resources.

The Tena Bar find is important to understanding what happened to Cooper after he left the airplane. If Cooper died in the jump, a hypothesis I reject, the simplest explanation for why he was not found is that he landed in the Columbia and his body was eventually swept into the Pacific Ocean. According to body recovery expert I've talked to, if Cooper landed in the Columbia his body would have sunk to the bottom very quickly; the water temperature was around 10C. Cooper's body would have "popped" to the surface sometime in the spring of 1972. This would give us the approximate layer of sand the money would have been found in, and would thus be a falsifiable theory.[19]

Regardless of what happened to Cooper, the money must have separated from him at some point, since no evidence of Cooper was found during the Tena Bar dig. We know money sinks once fully saturated with water, yet the ransom money was found well above where the river levels were at the time of the hijacking. In fact, it wouldn't be until 1972, then once again in 1977, when the river levels were high enough to match where the money was found. Since there is very limited real estate in the area where a body could rot and go unnoticed, the "Cooper died" hypothesis requires a search for mechanisms to get the money from the

---

[19]Palmer believed the layer of sand the bills were found in was a recent layer, well above dredging material from 1974. Kaye believes the money arrived earlier than the dredging spoils. Chemical evidence suggests the money may have been in contact with the dredge spoils for a long time. It may prove impossible to figure out what layer the money was truly in since no samples of Palmer's layers were kept.

bottom of the river to Tena Bar.

Because the Columbia is an important shipping lane, the river is regularly dredged. And there was a significant dredging operation a few years after the Cooper hijacking, in 1974. The big question is whether this dredging brought the money to Tena Bar. While this is a huge and ongoing topic of debate, the answer to this question is probably not. Dr. Leonard Palmer, the expert the FBI brought in to help unravel this mystery, dug a large trench near the money location. He determined the money was in a distinct layer that was well-above the 1974 dredge material. From "The Palmer Report" we get the "Washougal Washdown" theory that describes the money being somewhere upstream until the 1977 floods, which then brought the money to Tena Bar.

Tom Kaye re-examined Palmer's report and believes Palmer misidentified at least one of the layers from his trench. Kaye found a base layer of clay material running along the entire length of the sandbar. This layer appears to match the description of Palmer's clay layer, which Palmer concluded came from the 1974 dredging operation. Since Kaye found this clay layer along the entire length of Tena Bar (which was heavily eroded by this time), he concluded the clay layer was a natural formation and not from the 1974 dredge operation.

Kaye also looked at old photos of Tena Bar from before and after the '74 dredging and concluded the money was found a significant distance away from the dredging spoils, eliminating the dredge as the mechanism for getting the money to the bar. From this and his other findings, Kaye believes the money found its way to Tena Bar before the dredging operation. He even speculates some of the dredge material could have been pushed north by natural processes and thus helped cover the money until it was found.

Even if the dredge theory can be salvaged, despite two experts looking at the problem thirty years apart, it still doesn't necessarily help us in understanding what happened to Cooper. All it tells us is the money separated from Cooper sometime after the jump, somewhere near a watershed that feeds into the Columbia River.

On Tena Bar, the money was found at what many forum members believe was a "collection point" on the bar, where debris would gather during floods. The money location was near heavy foliage which would act as a natural backstop for debris. Since sandbars are dynamic environments, debris could be deposited on top of the sand and later be buried by wave and tidal action.

Something we can be certain of is that the money was put where it was found by natural forces. The evidence is overwhelming: the money was not planted at Tena Bar. Several FBI agents reported finding fragments during the dig. The size and distribution of the fragments is open to considerable debate, but there were fragments and this alone contraindicates human action. The state of the money reflected long-term exposure to the elements. The money was found in a spot where we'd expect to find flotsam to accumulate, and it was found downstream from where the 727 flight crossed the Columbia. Perhaps the only non-natural explanation for how the money got to Tena Bar is that Cooper, or someone else, threw all or some of the money into the Columbia at some point after the hijacking. I reject this out of hand, since the FBI did not reveal they had a record of all the serial numbers from the ransom money for about two years. As far as Cooper was concerned, the money was spendable. There's no reason to toss spendable money, especially after risking your life getting it.

The Tena Bar find has been an obsession for most of the members of the Cooper Forum, and represents the plurality of the posts found there. The focus spins around the three main theories 1) the money landed near Tena Bar, somewhere uphill and upstream, 2) Cooper and/or the money landed in the Columbia, snagged somewhere underwater, and some of the money was deposited via dredge, or 3) the money landed farther downstream, possibly in the Washougal watershed, and was delivered during the 1977 floods.

No single theory has gained traction. Each has strong evidence working for and against it. What does this all mean for the Gunther Hypothesis?

Given the provisional assumption that LeClair lost *a bag* of money, we can deduce one of several possibilities: The money may have fallen off of LeClair right away as he tumbled from the plane; the bag could have torn away from him during the opening shock of the parachute; or the money was lost at some point during LeClair's hard landing and he was unable to locate it in the darkness. Gunther makes no claim regarding a plant, and leaves us with the impression that the money Cooper landed with did not venture far from the landing zone. If anything, Gunther appears to be just as bewildered by the money find as the rest of us.

As a consequence, the Tena Bar find helps to indicate where LeClair either left the aircraft or where he landed or some point in between:

– If the money lands near Tena Bar or Caterpillar Island, LeClair lands somewhere in Salmon Creek or even Whipple Creek. This almost matches the description of LeClair's landing spot from the book. However, it requires moving the flight path west of where the FBI map indicates. (The "FBI Map" is another controversial topic. Many claim, most notably forum member Robert "Robert99" Nicholson, that it can't be 305's flight path.)

– If the money lands along the shores of the Columbia south and east of Tena Bar, Cooper lands in the Vancouver suburbs. This is generally not supported by the Gunther account. LeClair is said to have landed in a rocky river bed, not a suburban neighborhood. However, Clara's "cabin" is described more like a regular residential house than some rustic log cabin deep in the woods. The location of Clara's home is probably fabricated to protect her identity. Gunther suggests Clara was living in a house on Lake Merwin.

– If the money lands farther east, near Fifth Plain Creek, or Lacamas Creek, or somewhere in that watershed, Cooper lands in the same area or in an even more remote area of farms, forests and cabins. This almost exactly matches the circumstances from the book and does not require substantial deviation from the published flight path. However, it's difficult to imagine the money making its way from Lacamas creek, through Lake Lacamas and over a dam, and into the Columbia. Lacamas creek does not appear to have a strong enough current to carry bundles of money or a heavy money bag. Field testing on Lacamas creek would need to be done in conditions similar to the 1977 floods to see if this circumstance is tenable.

We can't be certain of any scenario since Gunther made changes to the story to protect Clara's identity. It's likely all the information regarding where the cabin was, how far Cooper traveled from his dropzone, how far the cabin was from any particular area, and where Cooper cached his equipment, are fabrications. This will make it nearly impossible to identify Clara from this information. However, based on the Tena Bar find, we can safely move Cooper's dropzone well south of Ariel, Washington.

The Drop Zone

The primary paradox in the Cooper case has been the discrepancy between the Tena Bar find and the FBI's original search grid near Ariel, Washington. From the FBI search area, water flows to the Lewis River in Ariel, where it dumps into the Columbia River, several miles downstream from where the money was found. The money would not move upstream on its own, so something has to give, either the money was moved by someone or the FBI got their search grid wrong. If you move the drop zone, it has to be moved a considerable distance in order to get the money upstream from Tena Bar. This has led to numerous theories, including the infamous Washougal Washdown theory.

I've mentioned the Washougal Washdown theory before, it's the FBI's current working theory based on The Palmer Report. The Washougal watershed pours into the Columbia near Camas, about 23 miles upstream from Tena Bar. This particular watershed covers a huge swath of relatively undeveloped forest that is located south and east of the original FBI search area. Most of this area is well east of the published flight path, and requires moving flight 305 outside of the Victor 23 air corridor. The theory is Cooper landed somewhere in this watershed, probably died, and the money was eventually grabbed by heavy flooding in the area in 1977. It would then make its way to Tena bar after the bag broke open. This theory has a few big problems. This area has now been searched by many people over the last 35 years and nothing of Cooper has been found. It requires moving the flight path by quite a bit. The rivers in the area were tested by Tom Kaye and he found that bundles of money do not stick together for the entire trip. A heavy bag of money would be even less likely to move down these streams. Most serious researchers no longer believe it to be a tenable explanation of the Tena Bar find. As such, we can't use this theory to estimate Cooper's landing.

I believe it is a mistake to use the Tena Bar and only the Tena Bar find to estimate a drop zone. Arbitrarily changing the drop zone based only on the find is a fallacy since we don't know how the money got there with 100% certainty. There is room for mechanical and human intervention in how the money was transported from its original starting position to Tena Bar. I prefer simpler explanations, but nothing is off the table. We can use the Tena Bar find as part of the equation, but first we need to look at what the available evidence was before little Brian Ingram found the money.

The timing and location of the jump could probably be pinpointed with the original radar information and data from the flight recorder but neither source is available anymore. Finding the true jump point will have to be made from other evidence, including eyewitness accounts. For simplicity, until other evidence is found which calls into question the original flight path, we shall adhere to the pre-existing evidence regarding where and when Flight 305 was during the times mentioned below. The key to eliminating the paradox is working the original evidence and finding out why the authorities calculated a drop zone near Ariel and why that was or was not in error.

Oscillations and the Pressure Bump

The main confusion in the eyewitness reports is whether there is a difference between the reported "oscillations" and the "pressure bump" caused by the stairs snapping back against the fuselage when Cooper jumped. Strictly speaking, we can't be sure there were two separate events. We know the pressure bump happened because it had to, testing showed this was the case. Rataczak, hand-flying the plane as it slowly flew through icing conditions, should have felt the disturbance in the airflow as Cooper crept out over the stairs. Cooper's movements inside the plane would not cause the 125,000 lb aircraft to change its trim, but the airstairs sticking out into the airstream would. Complicating this situation, turbulence could also bounce the plane around. As low as they were over the mountains, orographic disturbances could also cause the plane to bounce, even with light winds. Whether Rataczak reported the oscillations, the pressure bump or turbulence at 8:11pm on that night, we can't know.

We do know the cockpit crew keenly felt something. Anderson, the flight engineer, had pressure gauges on his panel and they would have jumped around significantly during the pressure bump (though he would have to be looking at the gauges when this happened). The pilot would need to trim the aircraft after Cooper left. The entire crew would have experienced ear popping from the momentary change in pressure. These pressure events were used in later hijackings to pinpoint landing zones for Cooper copycats like Richard McCoy. The entire narrative here is undocumented, and we only get after-the-fact recollections.

For our purposes, we're going to assume two distinct events. An oscillation which caused Rataczak to remark Cooper was "doing something with the air stairs" and was relayed over the radio around 7:11 pm, and a pressure bump caused by Cooper's jump sometime shortly after that.

The Evidence:

– At 8:11, the cockpit reported Cooper was possibly "doing something with the stairs" and relayed this information over the radio. It was overheard by a number of independent witnesses who were listening to these exchanges during the hijacking. This is the time generally given for the jump. In the released flight transcripts, nothing of consequence is communicated for the previous six minutes, indicating this was the beginning of the jump 'episode,' not its conclusion.

– Harold Anderson, the flight engineer, said the time of the bump was not recorded, but that it happened "five to ten minutes" after the last communication with Cooper, a time generally given as 8:05 pm. This would give an approximate range of 8:10 to 8:15 for the jump, plus or minus a minute.

– In the summaries of the crew debriefs, documents available on the Cooper Forum website, Anderson says the pressure bump occurred when 305 had "not reached Portland proper but were definitely in the suburbs or immediate vicinity thereof."

This gives some absolute barriers, Cooper did not leave before 7:10, and he was definitely gone by the time the plane was over

Portland. Another clue comes from the Time Table on Sluggo's website, which gives us this little tidbit:

SEA CNTR advises Portland Altimeter (Corresponding Sea Level Barometric Pressure) is 30.03 inches of Hg. [This is important because it shows that at 20:15:56 they were very near Portland.]

Finally, "Shutter" (owner of the DB Cooper Forum) has been working on the problem of the flight path with what I'll call "an extreme simulator" and did a test run from Ariel to Portland at my behest under nearly the same meteorological circumstances (he removed the cloud cover) and plane configuration of NWA flight 305. For my purposes, this simulation was mostly to get a view from the cockpit to better understand Anderson's statement about being near Portland. This is not a definitive test, you can see up to forty miles at 10,000 feet making Anderson's statements difficult to interpret.

My judgment, based on the simulation, is the absolute earliest someone from the cockpit could reasonably say they were near "Portland proper" is about five and a half minutes south of Ariel. This happened about 8:15 pm according to the published flight path. This is open to interpretation, and I encourage interested readers to see the video for themselves on the Project 305 YouTube channel.[20] I'm being very conservative with the estimate, and I believe this to be the northern barrier for the drop zone.

All the evidence appears to overlap around the 8:15 mark. This is the upper limit of Harold Anderson's statement of "five to ten minutes" after the 8:05 communication. At this location the flight was plausibly near enough to Portland both by my visual estimate from the cockpit simulator and from the communications transcript.

It can't be known exactly where 305 was at this instant, but the released FBI flight path suggests it is near Orchards, WA. It would be fair to say the flight could be plus or minus three miles north and south (one minute flying time), and perhaps one mile east and west from that point. This is significantly south of Ariel, very near the Lacamas River watershed, and it also makes a jump point over

---

[20] https://youtu.be/Mc7N5VqdbD0

the Columbia River a possibility (though our estimate here is still a few miles and about a minute of flying time short of the Columbia).

Sluggo's Flight Path Analysis

Admittedly, the statements from the crew are ambiguous. None of the crew have spoken definitively on the flight path or about the pressure event. Only Rataczak has regularly spoken publicly about the hijacking, and his remarks on the subject have been anything but clear. A strict interpretation, which is what others like Tom Kaye have favored, gives us the Ariel jump zone. By allowing for the possibility of two events and using the Ariel location for the start of the oscillation and using other evidence to establish the pressure bump, we get a drop zone farther south, closer to Portland and the Columbia River. This eliminates the paradox between where Cooper jumped and where the money was found, and does so without relying on the money find itself.

Here is the entire paragraph from the FOIA document:
"*Anderson stated that approximately 5 to 10 minutes after the last contact with subject at 8:05 pm, they heard and felt an oscillation of the aircraft and commented that the hijacker could have departed causing the unusual vibration since there had been no change in flight parameters or any other external force which would account for this sudden vibration. They telephoned the company representative (redacted) shortly thereafter and stated that the 'oscillation' which could have been the hijacker's departure, would have occurred between 8:05 pm and their call to the company 5 or ten minutes later, the exact time being recorded in the company log. Anderson stated that they had not reached Portland proper but were definitely in the suburbs or immediate vicinity thereof.*"

Problems with the Gunther Text

If the evidence presented in the Gunther book is so strong, why do few people actually believe it? There are a number of reasons, not least of which is the lack of a real name for a suspect. We feel lost without someone to actually investigate. (The clues Gunther give us should be enough to find this individual, which will be discussed later.) This isn't, however, the primary reason people are skeptical of the story. Gunther gets a lot of little details about the hijacking wrong as well. Gunther gets the seat and row Cooper sat in incorrect, Gunther writes about a confrontation between Cooper and 305 Captain Bill Scott when in fact Scott and the rest of the flight officers never left the cockpit. Entire chapters of Gunther's book appear filled with errors and misinformation (more on that later).

Most seriously, Gunther seems to contradict several important details of the hijacking that were kept secret by the FBI until only recently. These include the color of Cooper's parachute and the description of the bomb Cooper used. Gunther also gives us an apparently unbelievable account of how Cooper lost some of his money, and Gunther gets almost the entire hijacking narrative wrong. How do we reconcile these and all the other problems with Gunther's book if we are to take his story at face value? First, let's examine the major problems in detail.

Hijacking Narrative

There are problems with the entire hijacking narrative, mostly found in the second chapter of Gunther's book. A sample of these issues: Cooper never asked for a specific seat, the flight had an open seating arrangement. Gunther gets the seat row and number wrong. There is no mention of Bill Mitchell, the young college student in the row across from Gunther. Captain Scott never left the cockpit to talk to Gunther, nor did any of the flight crew. Cooper never asked where the plane was before he jumped. Cooper put on the parachute long before Mucklow was sent to the cockpit. These are just a few, Gunther gets a lot of little details wrong throughout this chapter.

It's actually not difficult to understand why. The primary reason is neither Gunther, nor Clara, were eyewitnesses to the hijacking. By the time Clara contacted Gunther, 'Dan LeClair' had been dead for several years. What little information Clara had came secondhand from LeClair. In fact, based on the text, it appears the primary recollection of the hijacking from LeClair's perspective was the unusual connection LeClair made with Tina Mucklow during the course of the hijacking. Otherwise, the hijacking narrative itself has been reconstructed based on Gunther's independent research. And it's possible his research was rushed, or he was fed misinformation.

This invites the question of why Clara didn't know more about the hijacking. She spent years with Cooper and it was obviously a major topic of discussion between the two. The only explanation is that she wasn't there. She didn't commit the hijacking, and she wasn't aware of what details Gunther or the FBI were really interested in getting from her. Why would she ask what seat Cooper was in? Or when he put the parachute on? What would she know about the fake bomb that she never saw? These details are important to the investigator, but not to anyone else. Gunther fills the gaps the best he can, using his own research to supplement Clara's story. The result is a mess; but it hardly disproves her story.

The Bomb

Gunther, presumably from Clara, describes the bomb as follows:

He found an attache case or small suitcase in a storage room at the hotel. Inside this case he built a fake bomb of red-painted tin cans, aluminum and wire (p. 137).

Here is how the bomb is described by eyewitness:

"In the left corner had 8 long sticks of about 6 inches long and 1 inch in diameter there were two rows of them. Then a wire out of there. Then a batt lite [sic], (probably like) a flashlight batt only as sthik [sic], (probably thick) as

my arm and eight inches long". [From RTTY or TTY Log Page 104]

Commonly, it is assumed the reddish sticks were road flares, wrapped around a large cell battery with black tape, plausibly accessorized with myriad wires to give the full "electric and technical" effect. I found Gunther's description of the bomb one of the more jarring and obviously erroneous passages in his book when I first read it.

However, it's actually plausible. LeClair was described as quite handy and mechanically minded. While I first thought of just regular cans of soup being spraypainted, it's possible LeClair may have removed the bottom and top pieces of several tin cans, rolled them tight and narrow to make the 'dynamite' sticks, then used an unmodified can or cans painted to look like the battery, and added the wires. Honestly, this doesn't seem a likely scenario given the availability of road flares and radio batteries. Since the bomb was never recovered, we can't know anything for certain. Personally, this description seems like it was mostly conjecture and misunderstanding on Clara's and Gunther's part.

The Money

This is especially complicated. Any Cooper story needs to account for the Tena Bar money find. We'll examine the finer details of how LeClair could lose part but not all the money in a later chapter. Here I just want to mention one of the biggest problems with the Gunther text. Several times, Clara claims LeClair specifically requested $20 bills. It appears from the text Clara really believed this, however we know Cooper did not specify any denomination for the money. This contradiction cannot be easily resolved, but I would say this mistake in the narrative from Clara evolved from Clara and LeClair's efforts to launder the money after the hijacking. Clara remarked how much easier it was to get rid of smaller denominations than larger ones. My guess is she projected this thought to LeClair and it became part of his "plan" after the fact.

Parachute Color

The traditional story regarding the parachute rig used in the Cooper hijacking was that he got an old Navy NB-6 container and harness with a 28-foot round canopy, and that the canopy was white. Over the years the details have changed depending on who and when the details were being discussed. Most recently, evidence was found by Cooper researcher Bruce Smith that Cooper likely used a Pioneer Parachute owned by an acrobatic pilot named Norman Hayden. Confusion over the ownership, type and color of the parachute used by Cooper is now an open question, at least until the FBI releases their complete files on the case. Even still, this may not help us learn whether, in the confusion on the night of the hijacking, the true color of the parachute was recorded. (In fact, opening the parachute container would have been both difficult for an amatuer and dangerous, as an improperly packed parachute can kill.)

Gunther, from Clara, describes the parachute as a multi-colored parachute with bright red and yellow panels. A quick Google image search for "Pioneer parachute" did return a vintage photo of a round canopy with black, red and yellow panels, so the color scheme itself is plausible.[21] Clara might not have seen the complete parachute before it was destroyed either, so it's possible there were more than two colors. Or, it could be a false recollection, or a Gunther fabrication. Who knows? Even ignoring the Gunther text, the parachute rig and ownership has turned into its own little mystery. The point here is not whether we can come to a definitive conclusion, the question is whether we need to explain every little contradiction or fuzzy detail completely.

The answer to that question is, basically, no we don't. What we have here is eyewitness testimony given over a decade after the events unfolded. The testimony is incomplete because our witness,

---

[21] This parachute color is even more plausible if Cooper really did jump with a NB6 or NB8 parachute that had a Steinthal C-9 canopy. A Google image search shows many multi-colored Steinthal canopies very similar to what Clara describes. Also, Thomas Colbert in his book "The Last Master Outlaw" claims the parachute had the color scheme Clara described. This detail comes up in a part of the book where FBI Special Agent Gary Tallis is being interviewed. It's unknown where Colbert or his co-author got this color scheme, but if it comes from Tallis it is a tremendous confirmation of the Gunther text. Colbert and his co-author were contacted about this, but they did not surrender the source.

Clara, wasn't on the plane. What she knows of the hijacking and how Dan LeClair planned it all is hearsay. Even events she witnessed could have been tainted by later events. For instance, it was her belief that Dan LeClair was a meticulous planner who would never leave anything to chance. This attitude likely influenced her belief that LeClair asked specifically for twenties when we know Cooper made no demands about the denomination of the currency.

We must also remember this book is much more than just the story Clara told Max Gunther. Gunther did his own research, including dozens of interviews with many of the principals in the case. He talked to several FBI agents, and had more than one interaction with Ralph Himmelsbach. Skipp Porteous talked to Himmelsbach about Max Gunther and relayed this exchange through his book "Into the Blast":

When I asked his opinion on Max Gunther's book, Himmelsbach said he didn't like Gunther and knew all about the book. He pointed out that Gunther claimed someone named 'Clara' talked to him and provided him with all the details about Cooper. Himmelsbach says that Gunther later changed his story to match the facts.[22]

This is an interesting exchange. It shows Gunther was doing research beyond what Clara told him, which tells us Clara's story was incomplete. The problem is we know nothing about what Gunther and the FBI agents discussed. I think it's very possible the FBI agents, maybe not Himmelsbach, gave Gunther false information as a way to test the story. [Law enforcement lying to journalists is so common that it is actually a topic of discussion in "Ethics in Crime and Justice" by Joycelyn Pollock, a textbook on ethics in law enforcement] This is where I think the confrontation between Captain Scott and Cooper comes from, misinformation given to Gunther to test the veracity of Clara's account. This is a common police tactic; they want their suspects to reveal information that wasn't public to prove a suspect's guilt. We simply

---

[22] Porteous, Skipp; Robert Blevins (2011-01-06). Into The Blast – The True Story of D.B. Cooper – Revised Edition (Kindle Locations 1043-1045). Adventure Books of Seattle. Kindle Edition.

can't know for sure whether this is the case here, but it goes a long way in explaining why Gunther's second chapter, and only this chapter dealing with the actual hijacking, is so full of errors.[23]

Gunther's book is a complex document. It is not just the eyewitness testimony of a single individual. It is very likely the story Gunther got from Clara was incomplete, and he was trying to fill in the gaps to create a narrative he knew his audience would expect from such an exposé. Gunther was a journalist; he was comfortable doing interviews and research. If you read through the book, you'll note he almost always references sources of information in the text. Once you start looking for them, you can source almost the entire book. He even hints in the text when he's just guessing about information. He uses phrases like "LeClair must have been thinking" or "LeClair probably did/thought/planned/etc."

Thanks to Gunther's habit, we can look at chapter two and source the problems. As it turns out, it looks like my idea about the FBI giving misleading information was correct. Gunther talked to several agents in addition to Himmelsbach, and it appears many of the factual errors were intentional misinformation.[24] This includes the prominent (and fictional) conversation between Cooper and Captain Scott. Providing false information wasn't a terrible idea on the FBI's part, but by this time Clara had broken off contact with Gunther and she would not have been able to correct the misinformation anyway.

If you're looking for a reason not to believe Gunther's story, you will find it. When first reading through the text, my primary goal was to find a reason to discount the story and move on with my investigation. And in my mind I had eliminated this story and was reading the rest of the book just to be thorough, until I eventually reached the point where Gunther revealed LeClair's profession. This fact, which represented the only time after-the-fact forensic evidence confirmed a DB Cooper confession, required a

---

[23]There is very little information from Clara in this chapter, based on the in-text sourcing, it is almost entirely based on Gunther's independent research.

[24]An interesting example of this is the give and take regarding the color of Cooper's tie. Gunther's interviewed Seattle Office Special Agent J. Earl Milnes about the tie, and he gave several different answers to the question, all supposedly reported by eyewitnesses. We now know the FBI had the tie, and Milnes would have known its actual color. It's obvious now that Milnes was trying to confirm Gunther's story. Unfortunately, Clara would have never seen the tie, and she never claimed to have seen the tie.

deeper look into the text. Upon close examination of the text, it is my belief, despite the aforementioned issues, that the Gunther hypothesis still holds true.

The Math of the Tie

It can't be emphasized enough how important the tie is to understanding who Dan Cooper was before the hijacking. Tom Kaye and his team found a family of particles that tells a distinct story about the life of its owner. The unalloyed titanium is one piece of the puzzle; Kaye also found other metals, including pieces of machined aluminum and steel, that point in a single direction: a metal fabrication shop making parts for use in industrial chemicals facilities. It's a specific enough lead to eliminate almost all of the existing suspects, and it can point us in the direction of finally solving this case.

Many in the Cooper world believe the tie Cooper left behind on the airplane could have been purchased by the hijacker from a thrift store. Indeed, because of the unique mixture of metallic particles on the tie, this assumption is often necessary to save their preferred suspect from being eliminated from the case. As such, it is necessary to ask whether it is plausible to assume the tie was purchased at a thrift store, and whether we can quantify how plausible.

At first glance it doesn't look so implausible. A tie picked at random from a thrift store had to belong to somebody, why wouldn't that somebody work at a metal fabrications shop in the industrial chemicals field? The odds of picking a tie belonging to a specific person are very low, but since every tie belongs to somebody with their own background and habits, it's possible Cooper's tie has nothing to do with Cooper himself.

However, we know Tom Kaye was able to connect the particles on the tie to Cooper's habits.[25] Kaye found the tie belonged to

---

[25]Kaye: "All of the stains examined showed elemental signatures of particles from safety matches similar to those shown in Figure 4. The stains, and in fact the Fig. 3 Comparison tie from the same period that had not been in storage for 40 years. Fewer particles are present on this tie even given its age. Fig. 3 Comparison tie from the same period that had not been in storage for 40 years. Fewer particles are present on this tie even given its age. vast majority of particles examined, had elemental compositions that were equivalent to match heads. This indicates that the owner of the tie was a smoker who did not typically use a lighter. Additionally, the type of match can be localized to paper book matches and not wood matches due to the lack of chlorine in wood matches [3]. These findings are completely consistent with the descriptions of D.B. Cooper as a chain smoker [4] that requested back the book of matches that the flight attendant, Tina Mucklow, used to light his cigarettes [5]." Retrieved from http://www.citizensleuths.com/uv-imaging-of-tie.html

someone who smoked a lot. Based on the density of particles found on the tie we know it was worn consistently over a long period of time... Yet the tie was only sold from 1964 to 1971. So there is a very limited window of time to get so much wear and accumulate all the particles evident on the tie under blacklight.[26] Certainly there wouldn't be enough time for one owner to use the tie and get exposed to a lot of metallic particles and another owner to blanket the tie in material associated with smoking. From a common sense perspective, it's safe to say the tie belonged to Cooper.

We can even try to calculate how unlikely it is Cooper purchased his tie from a thrift store. We know Cooper smoked and that 44% of men smoked in 1971. Cooper used matches from matchbooks to light his cigarettes. Once again, Kaye found particle evidence on the tie indicating matchbooks were the preferred ignition source for whomever owned the tie for those many years of wear before the hijacking. There is no data on ignition source preferences among smokers in 1971. I would guess it would be about half the population, the other half would use lighters or stick matches.[27]

Therefore, even though we can't get an exact figure, we can roughly estimate the probability of someone randomly picking a tie at a thrift store which matches their own smoking habits and preferred ignition source at about 22% (.44 times .5). Or, put another way, there is a 78% chance the tie belonged to Cooper long before the hijacking ever happened. If some evidence was found that Cooper was left-handed (other than the placement of the tie tack itself), we could be over 97% certain the tie belonged to Cooper.

There's another wrinkle here. Not only does the tie have to match Cooper's habits by chance, Max Gunther has to match Dan LeClair's career and life to what was later found on the tie, again by random chance. These are independent events, Gunther died long

---

[26] I now have the very odd hobby of seeking out old ties and looking at them under a blacklight. I have not found any tie with the density of particles found on Cooper's tie.

[27] This is just a guess, it's quite possible all smokers in 1971 used matchbooks at least some of the time. I use this number only to illustrate the potential to connect Cooper to the tie. The important part of this analysis is simply that we know the owner of the tie and Dan Cooper shared some pretty specific behaviours.

before the titanium was found by Kaye. There are two ways of looking at this question: one is through the real distribution of jobs, the second is by using the number of jobs Gunther could have picked from if he picked one at random from a list.

Using the actual distribution of the labor force, Gunther would have to pick a white collar job in the manufacturing sector. According to the 1970 Census, manufacturing accounted for 27% of the workforce. White collar work accounted for about 47% of jobs. Taken together, there is a 13% chance Gunther would pick the right kind job in the right sector. We'll use this as our low estimate.

It is unlikely, in my mind, that Gunther would be even thinking about the distribution of jobs if he were creating a fictional story.[28] Rather, he would likely choose from jobs he, as a journalist and author, would be familiar with. Likely, he would be familiar with many many jobs and careers as a financial writer. In the 1970 Census, more than 400 different jobs and careers are profiled by category and sector. If Gunther just picked something at random, we can safely say he had about 400 real choices.

On the conservative side of our estimate, there is a 13% chance Gunther picks the right sector and type of work, and there's a 44% chance Dan Cooper picks a tie at random that matches his smoking habit (ignoring, for a moment, the matchbook question); doing some basic probability calculations, there's only a 5.7% chance of these two events aligning in the way they have in this case. More realistically, we can say that there were over 400 possible careers for Gunther to choose from, and using the 22% estimate about Cooper picking a tie at random from earlier, we got the chance of these two independent events aligning at about 1.1 in 2000.

Yes, there's room to disagree about some of the particulars. You can adjust the parameters as you see fit. Regardless, this is a highly unlikely circumstance. We are asked to believe that Dan Cooper, living in the Pacific Northwest in 1971, bought a tie at a

---

[28] This is a major reason why I don't think Gunther is making any of this up. A novelist chooses the careers of his character for some specific purpose. He needs a rich character, or a miserable character, or some other quality to help move the plot. Picking industrial chemicals doesn't add anything to the character of Dan LeClair. If anything, his job is more interesting than the typical office drudgery I would have picked for a character who throws everything away to pursue adventure in a novel.

thrift store to wear on his hijacking and that tie would later prove to have particles that could have only been obtained in an esoteric industrial situation. Then we would have to believe an author living in Connecticut over a decade later would pick that same situation for his DB Cooper character in his book he was writing for the sole purpose of scamming money. Gunther was a long time journalist who would have been risking his professional reputation trying to commit such a scam. What side of the bet would you like to be on?

Surviving the Jump

Much of the debate in the DB Cooper case has centered around whether Cooper survived the jump. The weather wasn't perfect, Cooper was jumping at night with borrowed equipment and without standard skydiving gear or clothing. I've previously looked at this problem (my original paper is included with the Additional Materials) and came to the conclusion that the odds were in Cooper's favor even if he was an inexperienced skydiver. In my quest to understand the dynamics of Cooper's jump, I looked at bailout situations faced by bomber crews during the Second World War. I believe WWII represents the best place to look for such an analysis, as thousands of novice skydivers were forced to jump from stricken aircraft under extreme circumstances over unknown terrain, often at night, with unfamiliar equipment, in any weather situation and from a variety of aircraft speeds and configurations.

From all the situations I read about, combat bailout jumps were almost never made under ideal conditions (stable aircraft going less than 150 mph at proper altitude). In fact, there are some amazing tales of survival, including people who survived being thrown out of exploding aircraft, jumps made at very low altitudes (giving the flyers very little to no time to stabilize their bodies and pull the ripcord "by the book"), and with minimal training that was often, especially in the RAF, completely absent. There is a strong prima facie case for similarity between Cooper's jump and bailout jumps done in WWII.

Re-examination of WWII parachuting

In my original paper, I back-engineered a method for estimating Cooper's survival probability using the available WWII parachuting data, which amounted to comparing the number of airplanes lost (multiplied by the number of crew per aircraft) to the number of POWs held by the Axis powers. This gave an approximate survival rate of 80%. This process was done for several reasons, among them to save time, get a bigger sample size and because there wasn't an easily accessible collection of complete bailout data.

Unfortunately, aggregation of data at this level allows for a lot of variance. Confounds included not knowing the conditions surrounding every bailout situation, and the fact the number of POWs didn't necessarily represent the true number of survivors.

What was really needed was raw data from a large pool of actual parachuting events aggregated by a third party. In the process of finishing the first paper, I found just such an index. It was nearly complete and would give a good comparison between night and day jumps. Most importantly, it was not based on survivor self-reports, the information was third party and independently researched. Overcoming survivor bias is, in fact, the main problem this data set solved. If you use only self-reported survival stories, you automatically skew the data toward survival as non-survivors can't relate their experiences.

Further, the data is only from Denmark. Confining the events to a single geographic region helps control the number of variables; most importantly the civilian population of Denmark wasn't inclined to murder allied airmen like those in Germany.[29] In essence, this data from Denmark acts as a natural experiment to compare night and day jumps, and also gives us a healthy sample size from which to draw conclusions about Dan Cooper's survival.

The results

In 66 nighttime bailout events involving 210 jumpers, there were 192 successful parachute deployments for a 91.4% survival rate. There were 6 possible no-pulls, i.e. bodies found with undeployed parachutes, and 4 apparent parachute malfunctions (called "mals" among skydivers). For the daytime airmen, we have very similar results. In 46 situations, there were 244 airmen leaving stricken aircraft with 235 survivors on the ground for a 96.3% survival rate. We find four apparent parachute mals, but this time only one possible no-pull. The 91.4% survival rate for RAF airmen jumping at night is significantly higher than the result from my initial study, and it gives more credence to the possibility of DB

---

[29]There were many anecdotes about German civilians and SS troops executing downed allied airmen in the material I read for this section but Freeman Dyson discounts this as a major survival factor in his book "Disturbing the Universe".

Cooper surviving his jump.[30]

It needs to be stated that none of the possible no-pulls are confirmable. Injuries caused by enemy action could have prevented an airmen from deploying his parachute. There was no record anywhere in this sample of a group of men leaving an aircraft together only to discover later that someone didn't get a hand on their ripcord. There was a total of 454 jumpers between both groups, so the fact we have not one confirmable no-pull should be a significant indicator of how rare no-pulls must have been. There were tens of thousands of bailouts during WWII, so it's a near-certainty that some no-pulls happened. But I can't find enough information to get a baseline on just how often they occurred. Even using the number of possible no-pulls among the RAF in Denmark as a baseline for inexperienced night jumpers, we're looking at a rate of less than a 3%.

I ran a simple t-test comparing the US daytime and RAF nighttime samples; at a 95% confidence interval, the two samples are significantly different, but by an extremely thin margin. The difference between the two datasets was 4.88%, which is just a little higher than the 4.36% needed for significance. We can't be entirely sure of the cause of the difference between the RAF night jumps and the American daytime jumps. Not only did RAF bomber crews operate at night, they also had smaller escape hatches than American aircraft, and RAF crews often had to attach their parachutes before jumping, giving them less time to prepare for the actual bailout. Regardless, this data confirms the efficacy of the parachute as a life-saving device, and that amateurs and inexperienced persons can use this device with a high rate of success even under difficult circumstances.

Examination of No Pulls in Skydiving

Anecdotally, No-pulls are a common occurrence in sport skydiving. You can find self-reported examples and even videos

---

[30] It is my belief that there were no true "no pulls" during WWII. At all. Any airmen who jumped and was physically capable of pulling their rip cords did so. Any apparent "no-pull" would have been caused by wounds sustained due to enemy action.---MGAsr

with a simple search engine query. Skydivers even have equipment that automatically deploys their parachute if they haven't pulled their ripcord (or thrown their pilot chute) by a certain altitude. Skydivers take the possibility of a no-pull as a fact of their sport and have equipment and protocols to prevent fatalities caused by this phenomena. Since I couldn't find any anecdotes regarding no-pulls from my WWII research, I became interested in whether or not a no-pull is an inherent risk of parachuting in general, or if it is a byproduct of sport skydiving. To figure things out, I looked at the details behind all the no-pull fatalities recorded in the Skydiving Fatalities Database.[31]

Results:

There were 833 lethal parachuting incidents (skydiving is very safe, tens of thousands of jumps are done every year, almost all in ideal weather conditions)[32] catalogued in the Skydiving Fatalities Database between 1995 and 2009. Of these, 107 are classified as no-pulls. However, even among these, only 48 fatalities appear to be directly applicable to Cooper's jump. The majority of the recorded no-pulls involved demonstration jumps, group formations, camera work, health problems, suicides, or other situations that Cooper would not have been dealing with during his jump. Most of the no-pulls catalogued in the Skydiving Fatalities Database, and therefore most no-pulls from the world of skydiving, are caused either by the stunts and activities innate to the sport of skydiving, or by factors related to the mental or physical health of the skydiver.

Assuming Cooper was not suicidal, and there's no evidence he was, and assuming he didn't have a heart attack during the jump (admittedly, a real possibility for a middle-aged smoker in 1971), this greatly reduces the possibility of a no-pull situation during Norjak. When we combine this information with the WWII parachuting data, it becomes clear that DB Cooper had a very good

---

[31] http://www.skydivingfatalities.info/

[32] It must be noted, almost all skydiving fatalities happen in ideal weather conditions, making their safety record a little less impressive, in my humble opinion. ---MGAsr

chance to survive his jump. However, the database did show that six of the no-pull fatalities happened when borrowed or rented equipment was used, and one individual died while jumping at night; both of these risk factors were present during Cooper's jump but they represent a small minority of the total fatalities profiled in the database.

It will always be difficult to assess the true survivability of Cooper's jump since we do not know the extent of his skydiving experience, the state of his equipment, the configuration of the money and how it was attached to his harness, his mental state and his health. We can say with some certainty that the weather and the lack of daylight had very little effect on his survival. In all likelihood, from the broad perspective presented here, we can be about 90% confident Cooper pulled the ripcord on his parachute and it deployed properly. From there, we can only make educated guesses whether he was hurt on landing, or whether he lost his life by drowning in the Columbia River.

Losing the Money

Something that is very easy to do in this case is get lost in conjecture. In this book I have endeavored to stick as closely to the known facts of the case and not make any wild guesses about anything, and to focus on hard evidence. However, there is one area where the Gunther story and the Cooper story diverge, and that is in regards to how the money was lost, and what container it was in during the jump. In order to move forward with the Gunther Hypothesis we have to find some way to bridge the eyewitness testimony of Tina Mucklow on the airplane and that of Clara on the ground.

First, the best record of Tina's account of this issue can be found in the summary of her debrief interviews in the FOIA documents available on the Cooper website (emphases mine):

> *It was also during this time that he complained to Mucklow that he had requested the money be delivered in a knapsack but instead it was delivered in a cloth type bank bag, which displeased him. It was at this time that Mucklow recalls he stated he would be forced to use one of the parachutes to rewrap the money since he had not been furnished the knapsack.* **At this same time Mucklow says she suddenly observed him having a small green paper bag, contents unknown. She states that she recalled no other packages or luggage belonging to the hijacker except for the briefcase and this small green paper bag.** *She says it was also about this time she again offered the hijacker something to eat or drink, which he refused.*
>
> *Mucklow states that at takeoff from Seattle the hijacker was in seat 18-D or 18-E, occupying both seats at various times, and she was seated across the aisle in 18-C. Mucklow states that at takeoff the hijacker was using several seats and* **was occupied with opening one of the parachutes and attempting to pack the money in the parachute container and attach it to his body using the parachute (containers) straps.** *Mucklow recalls that the parachute was a bright pink-orange color. Mucklow's description is somewhat vague but she says he removed a small jack-knife from his pocket and he cut some portion of the outside container or the parachute in order to secure the money in 'this' rather than in the white cloth type bank bag which had been furnished him. She says that she did not see him tamper with the two large parachute containers other than to generally inspect them when she brought them aboard.*

This is from her 2nd interview:

> *After the passengers left Mucklow asked the hijacker if he wanted her to get the other items waiting outside and he said "yes", but he wanted the other crew members to remain seated. Mucklow then left and brought in one large parachute (back pack). The hijacker told her to lower the window shades, which she did. Mucklow then left again and brought in two small chutes (front packs). Her next trip she got the last 'big chute' and placed it with the others in Row 18. At this time Mucklow handed him a sheet of instructions on 'how to jump and use a parachute' and he said 'he didn't need that'. Prior to all of this Mucklow asked the hijacker if he wouldn't rather have one of the cockpit crew (men) get the chutes, but the hijacker told her 'they aren't that heavy and she wouldn't have any trouble'.*[33]
>
> *When Mucklow returned to the plane with the last backpack chute, she saw that the hijacker had one of the small chutes open and was cutting nylon cords out with his pocket knife. He took the nylon cord and wrapped it around the neck of the money bag numerous times and then he wrapped it a few times from top to bottom, and with the same piece (of cord) he made a loop like a handle at the top. This nylon cord was pinckish in color. He appeared irritated that they hadn't given him a knapsack for the money as requested, and* **after trying to put the money in an unfolded parachute, he decided to leave it in the canvas bag** *(and fabricate a holding line for that, instead).*

As soon as Cooper got the money, he was working on a solution to the problem of how to attach it securely for the jump. He apparently tried using one of the reserve parachutes as a container, and this didn't work. He used paracord to wrap the bank bag tight and make a handle to secure it to himself. We don't know exactly how he did this, but this is what Tina reported seeing. There is no reason to doubt her account.

One thing we do know is Tina said she saw a green paper bag. This is interesting because Clara says Cooper had stashed the money in a green canvas bag, which she later saw on the ground.

Here is what Clara relayed to Gunther (p 155-156):

---

[33] The hijacker knew this equipment was light. This is further evidence we're looking for someone with a parachuting background.

"When his foot repaired itself they went looking for the money he had hidden. There was snow on the ground. This changed the look of the land and confused him to some extent, but he had been careful to take note of distinctive trees and other landmarks and had frequently rehearsed the route in his mind." They were able to find the parachute, but the money bag was missing. They searched again but couldn't find it. As they ate some food they brought along, a raccoon watched them from a safe distance. "'That's it!' LeClair said. She frowned at him, not understanding. He said, 'That's where the money went! An animal dragged it off!'" LeClair had left some food inside the container with the money before he cached it.

A day or so later they returned to the original cache site and searched around the area. Eventually, Clara reports **they found the green bag,** *which had been ripped open by an animal. There was money still inside, and they found some other bundles scattered on the ground nearby. The total, when they took it home and counted it Was about $87,000. Adding that to the $16,000 already in hand, they now had some $103,000.*

When I first read this part of the book, I thought for sure it implied that the other $97,000 dollars had fallen out of the bag and had been spread across the countryside by the wind. But upon re-reading it, that is clearly not the case. A few bundles fell out of the bag, nothing more. Most importantly, I believe the green bag Clara saw and the green bag Tina Mucklow saw are the same item. I don't think Cooper had a green paper bag with him, a green paper bag is basically a unicorn, how often do you see one? Cooper had a small canvas bag with him, this is what the two witnesses saw.[34]

When I first began investigating the Cooper hijacking, before I was aware of the Gunther text, I felt Cooper lost the money when he pulled his ripcord. It was unlikely he'd be able to tie a knot with paracord that would hold under the strain of a hard parachute opening. Other hijackers lost their ransom in the air, and it took careful planning (notably from hijackers Richard McCoy and Robb Heady) to secure the money properly for such a jump. In the Gunther book, Clara claims that only half of the ransom was recovered. How is this possible? Either you lose the money, or you keep it. Certainly, losing half the money seems

---

[34]Technically, three witnesses, as passenger Nancy House also reported seeing a "burlap" bag, but she didn't remember it being green. It's also completely possible the green canvas bag Clara saw was the green reserve container, which could have been used to carry some of the money.

impossible.

According to Gunther text, LeClair brought a green canvas bag with him to help carry the money. Clara was sure LeClair had specifically requested twenty-dollar bills and had the bag with him for the ransom money. As noted previously, she was mistaken, as Cooper made no demands regarding denomination. The eyewitness reports show Cooper was flustered by the fact the money came in a bank bag instead of the requested 'knapsack,' this proves he had different ideas in mind for the money.

So why did he have this green bag? If Clara is right, Cooper brought the canvas bag for the money. It makes some sense, if he assumed he would be getting fifties and hundreds (not the twenty dollar bills he received), Cooper would have brought a bag big enough for between 2000 to 4000 bills. It would have been an easy enough backup plan in case he didn't get the knapsack he requested. We also know Cooper was very mindful about leaving any evidence behind. He collected all the notes from the flight attendants and he grabbed the empty matchbooks he brought with him. He took his briefcase, with the bomb. He took just about everything off the plane with him except his tie and cigarette butts. These wouldn't be useful to investigators until the advent of DNA testing decades later. Cooper having a canvas bag to attach to his harness for all the stuff he didn't want to leave behind would make complete sense.

Cooper Gets 10,000 bills

The money weighed about 10 kilos (22 pounds) and would have been bulky and difficult to deal with. It would also be very difficult to attach the bank bag to the parachute harness with paracord. The load would likely be asymmetrical, making Cooper unstable in free fall. Cooper's options improve if he splits the money between two bags. He can more evenly distribute the load on the harness. Ideally, he could fit half in his green canvas bag and leave the other half in the bank bag.

It is my belief this is what Cooper did. He attaches the two different containers to his harness and jumps out of the aircraft. When his parachute deploys, his canvas bag stays with him while the bank bag breaks away. Thus the bank bag, wrapped in paracord, was lost somewhere in the Columbia watershed or the Columbia River itself. It eventually gets sent down the river by the strong spring floods, possibly in 1977, and the money gets deposited by water flow on Tena bar. It's also possible the bag moved along the bottom of the Columbia, where it became part of the sediment layer that got removed by a dredge in 1974 and deposited on Tena Bar. (The actual mechanics involved in getting the money to Tena Bar are a guess, and it's such a huge point of contention in the Cooper world I don't want to state anything definitively. I do my best to tackle the Tena Bar problem elsewhere in the book.)

The three or four bundles of money found on Tena Bar could not survive in the elements unprotected for so long. They definitely wouldn't stay together and end up one on top of another on a sand bar without being together in the bag for a long time. The bills had to spend most of their time protected, and they must have traveled together in the same container to Tena Bar. Since nothing of the container was found, we must assume it broke apart at some point before reaching the sandbar. In all likelihood, the money had been together for so long it had clumped together in the solid mass it was found in. (I now tend to believe the money was in the container at the bottom of the Columbia and was brought to the surface by the 1974 dredge.)

Cooper using two bags for the money matches Tina Mucklow's testimony about the green bag, it explains at least in part the Tena bar money find, and it aligns with Clara's story. It is conjecture but it provides the simplest explanation for everything we know about the money found on Tena Bar.

Cooper's Home, Seattle or Portland?

When I originally started digging into the DB Cooper case for the short novella I wanted to write, I got stuck on an intractable problem. I couldn't figure out if Cooper was based in Seattle or Portland. Nor could I figure out if he wanted to land in Seattle or Portland. And I had no idea how he travelled between Seattle and Portland or how he intended to get back to his home. Based on Cooper's actions, it seemed like he wanted to bail out over Seattle. If so, then the FBI should have figured out how Cooper got to the airport in their investigation. They didn't, which means Cooper was probably based in Portland and didn't have to travel far or outside his normal routine. But if so, why did he then try to bail over Seattle?

To try to figure things out, I focused on where I thought Cooper intended to land. The resulting meditations led down a dark hallway of conflicting information.

It is my belief that Cooper must have had some kind of plan for his dropzone. The FBI does not think this; they believe Cooper was acting alone, that he was smart or clever, but not a mastermind. From their perspective, Cooper leapt out of that airplane without a clue where he was going to land... That he had put himself into a situation that was going to get him killed. Cooper did not communicate with the cockpit about the plane's position, therefore he must have been jumping blind and stupid.

This goes against everything we know about Cooper. Cooper made a bomb, real or not, that gave the impression he was a serious threat. He pre-wrote the first message he gave to the flight attendant, Flo Schaffner, which kept his handedness a secret. He then collected that note, and other evidence, leaving very little behind. We even know Cooper brought a knife, which allowed him to deal with the unexpected problem with the bank bag. This all signals planning. And not just a little basic planning, Cooper was ready for contingencies. I'm not suggesting Cooper was perfect or that he had the heist plotted out to the finest detail, but he did have a plan. He thought a lot about this. So where did he intend to land?

At first it seems obvious Cooper wanted to land in Seattle. We know Cooper asked to have the stairs down during takeoff. He put on the parachute harness almost as soon as he got it. The cockpit communicated to air traffic control that Cooper was trying to get the stairs down just seven minutes after takeoff. This suggests he wanted out of the aircraft, and soon.

Further, Cooper could identify Tacoma from the air and appeared to know the Seattle-Tacoma area very well (for instance, he know how long it took to drive from McChord Air Force Base to the airport). He knew Seattle in a way a tourist doesn't. This makes a strong case for Seattle being both Cooper's base of operation, his home territory, and his intended dropzone..

What about Portland? Why would I think Cooper was based here? Well, Cooper originally boarded the flight in Portland. The FBI tried to find out how Cooper got to the airport; they checked for abandoned vehicles, they interviewed cab drivers and bus drivers, but they were never able to figure anything out.[35] How Cooper got to the airport is a mystery. The FBI also looked into the hotels and motels around Portland and found nothing. Tina noted that Cooper had a matchbook from a company that had a restaurant in the Portland airport.[36] Did Cooper case the airport and plan his heist while enjoying meals at the SkyChefs restaurant at PDX? How did he get to Portland? Where was his car? What were his logistics and how did they stay so perfectly hidden from the FBI? The best explanation is that Cooper was from Portland.

So why was he trying to jump out of the aircraft in Seattle? Round and round we go.

How can we unravel this issue? First, while Cooper did fight to open the aft stairs as soon as possible, he didn't jump right away. In fact, it took at least six minutes for him to jump after his last communication with the cockpit. This despite the fact it had taken him nearly twenty minutes to get the stairs down. He must have known every minute counted. In just those six minutes, the plane traveled about 18 miles. If he wanted to get out near Seattle, why

---

[35]Cooper almost certainly used the plentiful public transportation options in Portland at the time.---MGAsr

[36]Admittedly the company had restaurants at many airports.

let so much time pass? Based on my own analysis of the timing of the jump, Cooper probably landed in the Vancouver suburbs, well within walking distance of the airport where the whole adventure first began. If I had to pick a homebase for Cooper, based only on the above evidence, I would favor Portland over Seattle, despite Cooper's obvious knowledge of the Puget Sound area.

How does all this fit in with the Gunther text?

The book gives us a simple explanation: LeClair was in Portland. And he wasn't trying to land near Seattle or Portland. Rather, he was trying to land between them. LeClair was intentionally aiming for the forests north of Vancouver.[37] As a former paratrooper, he knew how to parachute into a forest. As a paratrooper, he would not have been bothered by jumping at night, His plan after landing was to rely on his experience as an outdoorsman and walk out of the forest a free man. Based on the text, it appears LeClair didn't believe law enforcement would be able to pinpoint his jump until long after he had made his escape.

Cooper living in Portland answers other questions too. The FBI never figured out how he got to the airport because he probably used the plentiful public transportation options. When checking on hotels and motels, the FBI probably checked the guest list, not knowing the man they were looking for might have been an employee (according to Gunther's book LeClair worked for a hotel, but it is a possible fabrication). Yet, even though LeClair lived in the area, he wasn't pinpointed by anyone who knew him because he was a transient visitor to the area, having lived there for less than a year (this is an estimate from the Gunther text). There were no roots for investigators to find.

The only question remaining was how LeClair knew so much about Seattle. I can't answer that, there is no information in the book that gives us any clue why that is the case. I can only speculate that he scouted everything out before the hijacking, or he

---

[37]This tells me the Dan LeClair, if he wasn't a smokejumper himself, must have known a smokejumper. They intentionally aim at certain pine trees, depending on the circumstances, making them the only parachutists I know of who willingly land in trees.---MGAsr

knew Seattle from prior business trips. It's possible Cooper lived in Tacoma, or was stationed at Fort Lewis or McChord AFB. We can't know everything. This is simply the nature of this paradox.

Why Didn't the FBI Catch DB Cooper?

This case is an outlier as it represents the only unsolved skyjacking in American history. The FBI were good at their jobs, they solved all the other air piracy cases, so why did Cooper escape justice? The common answer from the FBI and many Cooper investigators has been to say Cooper died in the jump, which would leave the FBI had no one to catch. This is the current orthodoxy in this case: An unknown individual, a loner with few social connections, boarded the plane, jumped with the money, and impacted somewhere in the Washougal watershed. The FBI may not have found his body, but they know he didn't escape with the money.

There are other explanations for why Cooper was able to avoid the FBI. In fact, Cooper would have been the only skyjacker who had a realistic opportunity to avoid justice because he was the first to actually jump out of the aircraft. Here's what he had going for him that night:

— The FBI, and others, did not expect Cooper to jump. Up to this point in history, all other airplane hijackings had similar modus operandi: the plane would be hijacked, then flown somewhere, often Cuba. From there, the hijacker would try to defect with the ransom money. All of them failed. (Humorously, the Cubans would arrest and imprison plane hijackers regardless of their Marxist views.) It wasn't even publicly known if an airliner could be jumped safely. Only a very small group of people at the CIA and Boeing knew the 727 was a safe skydiving platform.

— Cooper lucked out because no one knew how to estimate the dropzone. During the most important time of the heist, the 24 hours after the jump, the FBI had no idea where to look, other than a vague search area encompassing almost all of Cowlitz and Clark counties in Washington. Ralph Himmelsbach even flew his airplane south of Portland in the days after the hijacking, before testing confirmed the Ariel jump location. Later, based on this hijacking and later testing, investigators could pinpoint a drop zone within a few miles.

– Cooper's audacity resulted in what can only be described as a lethargic reaction from law enforcement. During later hijackings, the FBI created a chain of communication that activated search parties, roadblocks, helicopters and flares to a drop zone very quickly during a skyjacking. Richard McCoy, a Cooper copycat, could actually see the search operations targeting him as he was floating to the ground in his parachute. For Cooper, there was almost no ground operation on the night of the jump, and only a cursory search over the following week.

These factors gave Cooper the time he needed to make his getaway. If he did land south of the original search location, he literally had years before people would be on his trail.

Live or die, Cooper made no large purchases with the ransom money. He made no major mistakes prior to or after the hijacking. No one recognized him from the sketches; he was not missed by friends or family. Whoever he was, he had no one close to him who could or would identify him as the skyjacker. This is a significant indicator of his social status at the time of the hijacking, and any suspect has to match this particular situation.

Cooper and only Cooper, could have gotten away with this crime. He was the first guy to attempt such a heist, which was the primary key to his success, and he made no major errors before, during, or after the hijacking to get himself caught.

Finding Dan LeClair

It does us no good to confirm the Gunther hypothesis without finding out who Dan Cooper was, where he was from, and what happened to him after the hijacking. It may seem an impossible undertaking as we are given very few clues about the real Dan LeClair, and any or all of these clues may be purposefully false or misleading. Here's a rundown of what Gunther tells us about LeClair: He was born French-Canadian, later moved to Detroit, then to Newark, he enlisted in the Army during WWII and became a paratrooper, he went to college on the GI Bill, he went into sales for an industrial chemical company and later worked his way up to an executive position, he started a family and had two children, he left his family sometime before the hijacking. On the original DZ forum, "Farflung" showed the tie was sold between 1964 and 1971, so we can estimate approximately when he would have left his family around 1969. LeClair permanently left the grid using a stolen identity.[38]

The only clue we can be nearly 100% sure of is that Dan LeClair was a white collar worker in the industrial chemical field. According to Alan Stone at the 2011 Cooper Symposium (Smith, p150) there were only four places in the United States where Cooper could have picked up those titanium particles. This is the primary lead in the case, this is how we'll find Dan Cooper. Even if the Gunther hypothesis is wrong, this clue alone can solve the case.

Employment records from five decades ago are probably scarce to nonexistent. However, family photo albums from company picnics, surviving employees, company literature and other records are probably available. Publicity would be our most important ally; people need to know we're looking for these sources. The Cooper case has a good following, but the latest research needs enough media attention to produce leads. In photographs, DB Cooper would be easy to spot, his swarthy complexion and above average height should make him stand out in any photos.

If Dan LeClair really did have children like Clara claims in the

---

[38]This was the reason why LeClair contacted Gunther, as Gunther wrote the article about disappearing that LeClair ended up using to escape his marriage.

Gunther book, they would be in their 60's or 70's now and still quite capable of identifying our suspect. They might even provide some details of his life that we didn't get from Clara. There would be family photos and other documentation to prove the story. The greatest treasure would be to finally photo-match the tie. This would be quite easy, despite how common his style of tie tack was, because Cooper put the tie tack on from the left hand side.

There are other records to check as well. We have WWII enlistments and WWII casualty records, as well as about 20% of the service records from the war (the rest were destroyed in a fire). Military historians might be able to place LeClair in a certain military unit based on the clues given in the Gunther text. We can compare those records with Census data. The 1940 Census has been available since 2012 and all the records are digitized and available for searching. There are about 400 men born between 1915 and 1939 who were born in Canada and lived in Newark in 1940. If LeClair was really from NYC, the number increases to over 3000. It's a big list and would take a lot of work to vet all the details, but if any of the information from the Gunther book is true, a few names will stick as possible suspects.

If LeClair was not born in Canada, finding his true identity may prove particularly difficult. Being Canadian by birth reduces the number of people who could be LeClair by a factor of ten. If the French-Canadian lead turns out to be a misrepresentation by Gunther or Clara, only through the leads from the chemical companies will we be able to find viable Cooper suspects. I do hold out some hope that, sometime in the future, all records from that era become searchable by electronic means: Death in Absentia records, obituaries, military service records, etc. Unfortunately, this digitization is decades away from completion.

Why haven't we found Dan LeClair?

Dan LeClair left his family sometime before 1971 but after 1964. He should have been reported missing, or declared dead in absentia sometime before 1978. There would be records from this era if he was declared dead, but they might not exist anymore. We also need to understand the difference between someone "missing" and listed in the missing persons database (NamUS), and someone declared dead in absentia. According to Wikipedia, between 60,000 and 100,000 people were declared dead in absentia in the US before 1990. The missing persons database is much smaller, just short of 23,000 cases are listed. "Death in Absentia" is a legal process, while the missing persons database specifically exists to find missing people, meaning the family of the missing person wants to find them. The fact our Dan LeClair did not end up in the NamUS shouldn't be very surprising.

Dan LeClair was never really missing. He left his family and they knew it. Based on the Gunther text, most of the family didn't really miss him either. The book says LeClair's wife attempted to have him declared dead. However, we don't know if she succeeded. LeClair made contact with his daughter, and was apparently in regular contact with her. If she had been asked about her father during any legal proceeding, she most likely would have been compelled to disclose the contact they had made, under threat of perjury.

Part of the process of declaring someone dead in absentia is detailed in Ross Richardson's book "Still Missing". (In the book, Ross profiles the case of missing person Dick Lepsy and connects him to the Cooper hijacking. Lepsy is profiled later in the book.) Ross shows us what insurance companies do to settle these claims out of court. Basically, members of the family are put under the threat of perjury and interrogated about their relationship with the missing person, and they have to declare that they are not nor ever have been in contact with the missing person since the date of the disappearance. There is followup as well. Ross details an unusual encounter one of Lepsy's survivors had when, years after the fact, they looked to see if Lepsy's Social Security number had any activity. Two men, claiming to be employees of the life insurance company covering Lepsy, investigated the incident. Mysteriously, the men were not actually employed by the insurance company and they have never been identified. (They were probably private investigators or bounty hunters monitoring a large list of Death in Absentia claimants sold to them by the insurance companies).

If Dan LeClair's wife tried to have him declared dead, they most likely went through this arbitration process with the life insurance company as described in Ross's book. I have to believe the results of the hearing would go against the LeClair family. If he had contact with his daughter, if it was known he was alive, he would not have been declared dead. The life insurance company would not have settled the claim. There would likely not be a record to search for, even if these records were still around. Finding LeClair through Death in Absentia records might be impossible.

Dan LeClair was, to put it bluntly, a deadbeat dad who left his wife and children. There's no heroism here, the wife would have been bitter about this. There would be plenty of resentment and ill will, and if the wife failed to get any life insurance money out of this event it would only add to her frustrations. There would be no legal Death in Absentia documents to find, he would not have been reported to NaMUS, and only his daughter would have had any contact with him after he went missing. The daughter would have known about his death, and that would have been the end to the family's interest in their father. Since the daughter would have had no idea LeClair was D.B. Cooper, she would have no interest in the case nor would she believe her mild-mannered father was the culprit. In fact, I wonder if she would believe her father was Cooper when presented the evidence today. Given these circumstances, it may prove difficult to find Dan LeClair's survivors even given ample publicity.

Conclusions

– Cooper's jump was very survivable. Based on data from WWII he almost certainly pulled the ripcord on his parachute. Emergency parachutes like the one Cooper used are very rugged and reliable, making a malfunction unlikely.

– Cooper probably did not land in the heavy forests north of Lake Merwin. Rather, he likely landed farther south, even as far south as the suburbs of Vancouver.

– DB Cooper escaped because he was the first to commit such a crime and law enforcement had no protocols to track someone jumping out of an airplane.

– There is strong circumstantial evidence the pseudonymous "Dan LeClair" from Max Gunther's "DB Cooper; What Really Happened" is really Dan Cooper.

– The most important piece of evidence is the titanium particles found on DB Cooper's tie that indicate Cooper worked in a very specific field before the hijacking. "Dan LeClair" is reported to have worked in this industry.

– The likelihood that Gunther's "Dan LeClair" would work in the industry most closely associated the rare particles found on the tie Cooper left behind on flight 305 are very low. This is evidence that wasn't discovered until long after the publication of Gunther's book.

– Max Gunther's book "DB Cooper; What Really Happened" provides a reasonable narrative of who DB Cooper really was, how he planned the hijacking, why he committed the crime, how he got away, and what happened to the money.

– "Dan LeClair" should be identifiable based on the information provided in Gunther's text. Tools such as the US Census, enlistment records, and the database of dead social security numbers can further the search for LeClair.

– None of the other publicly known suspects fit the evidence as well as Gunther's Dan LeClair.

The primary error for most researchers looking at this case is to find a suspect, normally someone who has led an interesting and adventurous life, and force the evidence to fit the suspect. It should be the other way around. The evidence should produce a suspect. Even though Dan Cooper didn't leave much behind for us to find, he left enough. We know where he must have worked before the hijacking, and what kind of work he did. This where any investigation into finding DB Cooper needs to start.

This book is about a suspect. Occasionally I have tried to understand how the suspect's story works with the evidence available to us, but the only reason we have delved so deeply into Max Gunther's "Dan LeClair" is because the suspect fits the evidence. Most importantly, this was evidence that was unavailable to Gunther when he published the book. The particle evidence on the tie is paramount in this case; I believe I've shown that it's very unlikely the tie was purchased second hand. If nothing else, common sense tells us the tie belonged to Cooper. Even more unlikely is that Gunther would select, from all the possible careers, the one industry where a white collar worker might get exposed to pure titanium particles like those Kaye found on the tie. The odds of these two independent events aligning is very low.

We can't keep chasing suspects because they are interesting people who led adventurous lives. We can't keep finding suspects based on "skill set" because there is an endless supply of them. Chasing the tie evidence will lead us to a suspect. I believe that suspect will be the man "Clara" talked about in her conversations with Max Gunther back in the 1980's. I could be wrong, but what's great about the Gunther hypothesis is even if Gunther really did make the whole thing up, we could find Dan Cooper anyway. There were only a few places Cooper could have worked and lived, and we can find him based on this alone. However, we should be confident in the Gunther text; besides the connection with the physical evidence, Gunther's book makes predictions that have passed the test of time.

In the book, LeClair destroys all the evidence. Gunther isn't specific, but presumably this means the parachute, the bank bag, the rig, and anything else LeClair thought might connect him to the hijacking, except the money. This isn't stated as a prediction, but it has so far remained true: Nothing of Cooper has been found since the publication of the book. No parachute, no clothing, no body, nothing has been found.

Clara and LeClair laundered the money many years after the hijacking, using casinos to trade their marked twenties for bankable cash. This is long after anyone would have been looking for it, and about forty years before people could check serial numbers on the internet. The life expectancy of a twenty dollar bill is about 8 years. The bills would have been well circulated to begin with, and would not have been culled by currency collectors. According to Clara, all the money was laundered, lost in the sea of casino cash. In the years since Gunther's book was published, none of the money has surfaced in circulation.

Gunther gives us one of the few Cooper stories that acknowledges the Tena Bar find in a realistic way. Basically, Gunther can't explain how the money got to Tena Bar. Clara can't. They don't even try. LeClair lost a little less than half the money in the jump. They don't really explain how, and that's that. There's no suggestion of a plant. There's no ridiculous story about trying to fool the FBI. There's no attempt to explain it except to say it got there somehow. It has taken a long time to definitively prove it, but the money got to Tena Bar--somehow--and was buried. It may have been through a mixture of dredging activity and natural processes, but the money wasn't intentionally buried on Tena Bar.

There are no extra quirks to Gunther's story. LeClair didn't try to meet with an accomplice on the ground. There wasn't a hidden vehicle. There's no complicated plan to trick people by pretending to jump at one point then secretly jumping later. The story is mundane from the start: an unremarkable but intelligent man spent months thinking through the heist like it was a mechanical problem. In the end, the man committed the hijacking, injured himself on the ground, and found help.

The tools exist, and will continue to exist, that will identify LeClair and where he lived and worked. It's called the U.S. Census, and once the 1950/1960/1970 censuses are digitized and databased, it will be a simple matter to cross reference military records with elements of the Gunther story and find a few good candidates to investigate. By 2040, this case could be solved without DNA, the money, the parachute or anything else.

I currently have a list of names of people who match some or all of the details Gunther gives us. What is of particular interest is this: there is only one person in the entire 1940 US Census who was 1) Born in Canada, 2) lived in Newark, NJ, 3) Enlisted in the Army in WWII, 4) Survived the war, and 5) was named "Dan" or "Daniel." This man is named Dan E. Clair, born 1919 in Canada. Since identifying him, I have been unable to find any other information about him. I'm not saying he is Dan Cooper, but he's at the top of a short list of people I'm trying to get more information on. To see the rest, please visit martinandrade.wordpress.com and click the "DB Cooper" tab at the top of the page for more information or to help in the search.

I have to emphasize, we don't know Dan LeClair's real name, we don't have pictures of him, we don't know where's he buried, or even if Dan LeClair really existed. I believe there is strong evidence that confirms the Gunther story about Dan Cooper being a middle-aged manager who left his family behind and hijacked an aircraft. The fact we now know what industry Cooper worked in, and thus where he could have worked from 1964 to 1971, means we can start pursuing real leads in the case. People need to know about this lead, and it's very unfortunate that this piece of evidence is not better known. It is the goal of this book to present to the public the only viable avenue left to find out who DB Cooper was and what happened to him after the jump. I leave it up to the reader to decide if I've accomplished this or not.

The Cooper Hijacking is solvable. Dan Cooper was a real human being with friends, relatives, coworkers, and a story. Given enough time and resources, I believe the case can be solved within the next few years. The most important tool will be publicity. We need regular people who lived near or worked at some of these industrial chemical companies to go back into their photo albums and other records to help us find the real Dan Cooper. Anyone who worked in industrial chemicals or with raw titanium in the late 1960's or early 1970's is encouraged to contact the author at marty.andrade@gmail.com.

Annotated Bibliography

Richard Tosaw, "D.B. Cooper: Dead or Alive"

Tosaw had extensive contact with Tina Mucklow, the principal witness in this case. After working with Tosaw on this book, Tina would not talk to another reporter or author again for three decades. Tosaw is not an objective source, he believes Cooper died in the jump (He would later spend much of his personal fortune looking for evidence of Cooper in the Columbia) and it looks like he got a few of his facts wrong about the hijacking itself. However, this book represents the only real chance to read about the hijacking from Tina's point of view, and as such it's an important resource.

Geoffrey Gray, "Skyjack"

This is the book I would tell people to read if they're just starting out .This book is fun and contains a lot of great information. Gray threads everything about this hijacking, the suspects, the characters, the principals, the obsessed investigators, and the whole media circus, into a wonderful narrative. The actual information about the hijacking tends to be superficial, and he gets a few things wrong, especially regarding the titanium found on Cooper's tie. Still, a great read.

Ralph Himmelsbach, "Norjak"

This is actually a strange book; Himmelsbach used a ghostwriter who switched between a third-person and first-person narrative. Parts of the book are obviously not Himmelsbach, to the point where the viewpoint is in direct opposition to positions Himmelsbach has clearly explicated in other media. Despite these faults, this book includes a lot from Himmelsbach. He was the FBI agent most associated with this case, and as such his is an important viewpoint to understand.

Bruce Smith, "D.B. Cooper and the FBI"

Bruce has been indefatigable in pursuing the principal witnesses of this case. He actively reports on all aspects of the Cooper world and the hijacking story. This book is probably the most comprehensive book ever written on the case. It includes almost all the publicly known suspects, extensive reports on the Tina Bar money find, the parachutes Cooper used, etc. It's the book I turned to the most as a reference during my investigation. Full disclosure, I did help Smith copyedit parts of the second edition.

Max Gunther, "D.B. Cooper: What Really Happened"

In ways that become apparent when reading it, this book is a mess. It's not a surprise it wasn't taken seriously when it was first published. Gunther padded much of the text because it appears the material he got from Clara wasn't enough for a proper book. His research was extensive, but occasionally haphazard. Gunther wasn't a crime writer, and he's out of his element. However, it's the real story of Dan Cooper, which is all it needs to be.

Skipp Porteous, Robert Blevins, "Into the Blast"

"Into the Blast" presents the circumstantial case against Kenny Christiansen, a suspect some will remember from Brad Meltzer's "Decoded". For the most part, there's nothing of interest to serious Cooper researchers to be found here. However, the authors did speak with Ralph Himmelsbach about Gunther's book and parts of that conversation are reported; Himmelsbach suggested Gunther changed parts of his story after talking to him and other FBI agents.

Ron and Pat Forman, "The Legend of DB Cooper: Death by Natural Causes"

This is a great little memoir on the life of Barbara Dayton, born Robert Dayton. Read as a book about a fascinating person who lived a life of adventure and mischief, it won't disappoint. As a book about the D.B. Cooper hijacking, it's less interesting. Dayton's confession of the Cooper hijacking is definitely false. Dayton moves the jump well-south of the Columbia River, and there's no explanation about the Tena Bar money find, etc.

Bill Rataczak, "Hijacked! D.B. Cooper and Northwest Flight #305"

An hour-long presentation from the co-pilot of Northwest Flight 305, this DVD from the NWA History Centre, is the only in-depth first-hand account available to us. "Rat" was at the controls of 305 when Cooper jumped. He talked directly to the hijacker (over the phone), and is a lifelong friend to Tina Mucklow. His account included interesting details of the hijacking that are found nowhere else. I found a copy on ebay; some clips have appeared on YouTube from time to time.

Russ Calame, "D.B. Cooper: The Real McCoy"

Richard McCoy was a popular Cooper suspect for a long time. He successfully hijacked his own 727 and parachuted into the Utah desert, only to be caught soon-after by the FBI. This book tackles the hijacking phenomenon from a law enforcement perspective, showing the reader how the FBI conducted its business in catching and prosecuting air pirates. It's a must-read for anyone looking into the Cooper case.

Ross Richardson, "Still Missing"

Dick Lepsy left his home to go to his job as a grocery store manager. He vanished, taking with him $2000 from his employers and nothing else but the shirt on his back. His car was found at a nearby airport. He has never been seen or heard from since. Ross gives us the rundown of this mystery, plus two others (one of which has since been solved) in this book. Ross connects Lepsy's disappearance with the Cooper hijacking. While I don't think Lepsy is Dan Cooper, his disappearance is worthy of attention as Lepsy left behind several children.

Tom Kaye, et al., CitizenSleuths.com

Former Norjak case agent Larry Carr opened up the FBI files and tried to crowdsource the Norjak investigation in 2010. Tom Kaye was one of the heavy hitters who took up the challenge, and it is Kaye who found the titanium particles on Cooper's tie. Kaye had access to the FBI files and investigated the flight path, the Tena Bar find and even looked at some of the actual ransom money. His conclusions regarding who Cooper was before the hijacking are used heavily throughout this book.

Thomas J Colbert & Tom Szollosi, "The Last Master Outlaw"

This book covers the life of Robert Wesley Rackstraw, the new-old suspect featured in the 2016 History Channel special on DB Cooper. Rackstraw has garnered a lot of attention thanks to the efforts of Colbert, an experienced TV man with an eye for a good story. The Last Master Outlaw presents the results of a multiyear investigation into Rackstraw's life and his connection to the Norjak case. The book is excellent, the level and quality of the research and writing is impressive. I disagree with Colbert's conclusions and believe his circumstantial case is no stronger than the circumstantial cases for other Cooper suspects, but Rackstraw makes for an interesting case study into criminal behavior. I highly recommend the book

Major Suspect Profiles

Over 1000 suspects have reportedly been investigated by the FBI since the night of the hijacking. The vast majority of these were cranks and false confessions. A significant number were felons serving time in state prisons who were trying to get into federal prisons (which were presumably nicer). A few suspects have caught the public's attention over the years. As part of my investigation, I looked into every suspect I could. The important suspects are profiled here, minor suspects that are still notable are profiled in the next chapter.

Dick Lepsy

One of the few "good" Cooper candidates from the missing persons database is Dick Lepsy. He left his wife and children a couple of years before the hijacking, and was never heard from again. Because he absconded, he was not listed as a missing person for many years. In his book "Norjack", Himmelsbach says the FBI took a very close look at all the missing persons who disappeared before the hijacking and came up with nothing. However, since Lepsy (and another Cooper suspect, Mel Wilson) weren't listed as missing at the time, the FBI never investigated either one as a potential Cooper suspect. (Wilson is an interesting case, one we'll look at a little later).

Ross Richardson's book "Still Missing" gives an overview of the Lepsy disappearance, including potential links to DB Cooper. While going through Lepsy's profile, we have to be mindful of the fact Lepsy left behind a family who never stopped looking for him. The recent media coverage outlining the possibility Lepsy was DB Cooper is great if it helps Lepsy's family find out what happened to him.

Ross presents a circumstantial case linking Lepsy to Cooper. Point number one is Lepsy's resemblance to the early Cooper composite drawing, and his physical description generally matches Cooper's. The second point is that Lepsy went missing a couple of years before the hijacking. And that's the argument. It seems like a thin case, but since there are so very few missing people who fit Cooper's description, Lepsy deserves a long look.

Lepsy was a grocery store manager in Grayling, Michigan. He had four kids and had been in a relationship with his wife Jackie since he was a teenager. At the time of his disappearance, Lepsy was probably cheating on his wife with someone from his work. Having been married at such a young age, it wouldn't be surprising. Lepsy might have been experiencing some form of quarter or mid-life crisis. Getting married very young, working an unremarkable but stressful job, raising four kids. It's understandable.

The current theory is he left everything behind except the clothes on his back and $2000,[39] and left on an airplane to Mexico with a young woman (who has never been identified, assuming the story is true). Such an escape to somewhere exotic would be an attractive proposition for many men, particularly one drifting through life, approaching middle age.

Lepsy has not been seen or heard from since the day of his disappearance. It's possible one of his friends, named in Ross's book, might have known part of the story. However, he never said anything, even when asked about it long after Lepsy's disappearance. Lepsy's car was found in an airport parking lot. While the rumor was he went to Mexico, his actual destination has never been known. It's possible he never got on a flight, as no one has been able to confirm he boarded a plane that day.

Other than matching the general physical description, what other elements of the Cooper hijacking does Lepsy account for?

None.

Lepsy had no knowledge of aviation, he was not a regular airline traveler. He would not be familiar with all the technical details about the 727 like Cooper seemed to be. Lepsy did not work in any industry that used unalloyed titanium, and thus he could not have been the original owner of the tie found on Cooper's seat. Lepsy had no experience in parachuting, skydiving, or even wearing a parachute harness. He was much younger than the median reported age for Cooper, he smoked the wrong brand

---

[39]This was not enough money to support Lepsy from his disappearance to the hijacking. He would either need a job, or he would need to turn to criminal activity long before Cooper boarded the aircraft.---MGAsr

of cigarettes, and he was not from, nor had he lived in the Pacific Northwest. He looks, on the surface, to be a poor suspect to be Dan Cooper.

Lepsy's "Black Box."

Any criticism of Lepsy as a suspect is generally answered with what I call the "Black Box" response. Lepsy went missing about two years before Norjak. Thus, he had two years in Mexico (or wherever) to plan out all the details and do all the necessary research for this hijacking. So the answer to any objection to Lepsy being Cooper is answered with "well, he learned it in Mexico." Here are a few examples to illustrate how frustrating this can be:

"Lepsy, a regular guy from the Midwest, would not use the phrase 'Negotiable Currency.'"
"He learned it going into and out of Mexico."
"Lepsy looks too heavy to be Cooper."
"He lost weight in Mexico, and got a really deep tan, and learned a little bit about skydiving, all in Mexico…"
"We have no evidence that he ever got to Mexico."
"We have no evidence he didn't get to Mexico"

Because we have no information about Lepsy between the date of his disappearance in October of 1969 and the Cooper hijacking in November of 1971, we can fill those two years with whatever we want or need to in order to match the details about DB Cooper noted by witnesses during the hijacking.

Might there be a way to bridge this knowledge gap? Some empirical way to connect Lepsy with Cooper without resorting to a black box argument?

Maybe.

The Secret Intellectual

Lepsy was an uneducated store manager who had no prior history of criminal activity. He looks like an especially bad fit for a crime such as an aviation hijacking. Norjack involved incredible panache and style, chutzpah, and loads of technical detail and careful planning. Cooper remained calm during the hijacking, he had a lot of technical knowledge about aircraft and airline flying, was familiar with the Seattle/Tacoma area, and he seemed completely comfortable wearing a parachute and jumping out of an aircraft.

Lepsy may not have been a criminal most of his life, but we have to note that he did embezzle $2000 from his store before leaving. We could say his life of crime began the moment he left his wife and kids. It would not be unreasonable to expect more criminal activity from Lepsy after his disappearance, especially if some kind of hardship set in. That original $2,000 (about $10,000 in today's money) would not have lasted very long. Turning to criminal activity makes sense.

What about all those technical details? How do we turn an uneducated grocery store manager into a criminal mastermind? It's not unfathomable. While Lepsy was uneducated, he was very well read. Very well read.

According to the settlement hearing transcripts published in Ross's book (his wife later tried to declare him dead for insurance purposes), Lepsy's most prized possession was a series of books by Will and Ariel Durant that gave a detailed survey of Western Civilization from an historical and philosophical perspective. (The last book in the series won a Pulitzer Prize.) I own this multi-volume work, and it is an exquisite review of western thought. It then comes as no surprise that Lepsy regularly read ancient Greek myths and plays to his children He was a regular reader of classic books and it appears he understood these books at a high level. Doubtless, Lepsy would have excelled at the humanities had he ever gone to college. This demonstrates Lepsy wasn't a dullard but a very intelligent and well-read person capable of thinking such a crime through in advance.

Other than the $2,000 taken from his employers, Lepsy had no other criminal history prior to his disappearance. In my view, this isn't a slam-dunk for the Lepsy hypothesis. Even though Lepsy took money from his employers, he could have stolen much more than that. He showed restraint and likely only took the bare minimum he needed to escape. It's even likely he only took money he felt was owed to him, for whatever reason, by the store. My guess is Lepsy rationalized the theft as some form of severance for the decade or so of dedicated service to the company.

Since the Lepsy-as-Cooper hypothesis is wrong on several fronts and the fact Lepsy fails to account for any of the pieces of evidence associated with the Cooper hijacking, I have to reject him as Cooper, despite his passing resemblance to the sketch and physical description. My conclusion, based on Richardson's book, is that Lepsy met with foul play sometime soon after he left. Lepsy was a committed father and it would have been, in my estimation, unlikely that he would have gone two years without trying to make some contact with his children.

To move his candidacy forward, there has to be some accounting for where he was in the interim years before the hijacking. If he was the hijacker, he must have turned to crime very soon after absconding. At some point, Lepsy would have needed to fly into SeaTac. At some point, Lepsy would have needed to either skydive or interact with skydivers. Lepsy would have needed to do research on the 727, so what reference material could Lepsy have found in libraries? Does that reference material tell him what the flap settings were? Richardson, posting on the Cooper forum, believes Lepsy "read up" on skydiving. Again, read what? What could you find in a bookstore or library that would teach him how to put on parachute harness with such ease?

Since both the Lepsy case and the Cooper case remain unsolved, it's alluring to try to solve one mystery with another. Unfortunately, there is simply no evidence linking Lepsy to Cooper.

Duane Weber

One of the most prolific posters on the original DropZone Cooper forum, and otherwise consummate Cooper gadfly, is Jo Weber. Well known to most of the independent sleuths of the case, she claims her deceased husband, Duane Weber, gave a deathbed confession to the crime, telling her he was "Dan Cooper" days before dying. This led Jo on the road to spending the next two decades investigating the case and her husband's checkered past. Her introduction to the Cooper case, at least after Duane's confession, came when she read Max Gunther's book, which was the only book on Cooper from her local library. It is at this point she started to make connections between Duane's life and that of "Dan LeClair."

She even claims to have contacted Gunther, convinced "Clara" (the woman who gave the story to Gunther) was an ex-girlfriend of Duane's.[40] She also contacted Ralph Himmelsbach, who either encouraged her or at least humored her enough for her to continue to claim Duane was Cooper. She was the catalyst to starting the Cooper thread on the DropZone forum, and posted nearly every day for seven years.

As interesting as her stories are, Duane Weber is not Dan Cooper. While he does roughly match the physical description, he's not particularly reminiscent of the FBI sketch. Passenger Bill Mitchell, who sat in a row across from Cooper, doesn't believe Duane was Cooper because he had comically large ears, something Mitchell would have noticed and remembered. Duane could not be put anywhere near the Pacific Northwest at the time of the hijacking, and there's no evidence he had any knowledge of the 727 or of the airline business in general.

The tie evidence also contraindicates Weber, since Weber never worked in any industry that used the spectrum of metallic particles found on Cooper's tie. Jo disputes this, I've now heard two explanations for the titanium: one is Duane worked in dentistry and would have had some exposure to titanium and other metals, the other that Duane sold nuts and bolts, some from Boeing. Both

---

[40] I have spoken to Jo about Gunther, and I believe she did have extensive contact with him. Unfortunately, she refused to show me any of their correspondence.

explanations are specious for a variety of reasons. Kaye has conclusively proven the particles are from a very specific industry. Finally, some of Duane's DNA was submitted for testing to compare it with samples taken from Cooper's tie. Those tests came up negative. The FBI spent considerable resources looking at Duane, and they do not consider him a suspect.

I created a spreadsheet with all the Cooper suspects and all the clues in the case, giving points when a suspect matched the evidence and taking points away when they don't. Pretty simple, somewhat subjective (and available on my website),but it really helps separate good candidates from bad. Duane Weber scores lower than every other suspect I've profiled. Duane Weber is not D.B. Cooper. In all likelihood, Jo internalized the Gunther story and used it as a platform to build up her own stories about Duane.

It appears as though she really did have significant contact with Max Gunther, and as such she could be an important source in helping clarify Gunther's actual contact with Clara, what research he did, and other important details that would help us better solve the case. I have spoken to her at length about Gunther and about Duane. It's clear from our discussions that she earnestly believes Duane is Dan Cooper. In the months before this book was published, she revealed Duane had family connections to the Pacific Northwest, and that he was possibly employed by the CIA. Her new evidence, none of which are falsifiable, fails to put Duane on Flight 305. She has had two decades to find a link between Duane and the hijacking, and has come up with nothing more than stories.

Duane Weber is not a viable Cooper suspect.

Sheridan Peterson

It's more difficult to explain why Peterson isn't Dan Cooper than to give the myriad reasons why everyone believes he could be the famed hijacker. To wit: Peterson was an experienced skydiver, he was trained as a smokejumper and pursued skydiving as a hobby. As a member of Boeing's fledgling skydiving club, Peterson did a skydive while wearing a business suit and carrying a heavy bag of flour (it was strapped to his body, and he did it to create a streak in the sky), a jump is very reminiscent of Cooper's. We can safely say he had the means and mentality to jump out of a 727 wearing a suit and carrying a heavy sack of money.

Sheridan worked at Boeing in the Manuals and Handbooks group, and he did so while the 727 was being put through its trials. He would have had the requisite aviation knowledge and the specific information on the 727 that Cooper appeared to have. Most incredibly, Peterson worked at Boeing at a time when abandoned mechanical equipment was left in large bins for employees to rummage through for their own use. Some of that equipment would certainly have been involved in the testing involving pure titanium being done at Boeing for the Supersonic Transport program (SST). This makes Sheridan Peterson the only candidate other than LeClair who plausibly accounts for the titanium particles found on Cooper's tie. Not surprisingly, he has remained a popular suspect. In fact, he is the only known suspect for whom there exists a plausible connection with Kaye's analysis of Cooper's tie.

Peterson had the dark complexion, receding hairline and basic physical characteristics of the hijacker. During his stint in Vietnam working for the State Department during the Vietnam War, he became disillusioned with the American presence there and became a lifelong anti-war activist, something he continues to this day. This gives Peterson a plausible motive for the crime. Other than having blue eyes, Peterson is a perfect fit. So perfect, in fact, the FBI pegged him as a suspect soon after the hijacking.

By all accounts, the FBI's Norjak investigation was thorough. If they suspected Peterson at all, they would have shown his photo to eyewitnesses. They would have looked into his whereabouts. They would have, and did, talk to family, friends and acquaintances. Nothing came of it, and Peterson has remained a free man. In 2002, his DNA was collected by the FBI and tested against the samples found on Cooper's tie. There was no match. After thirty years, the FBI completely eliminated Peterson as a suspect.

A lifelong peace activist, this crime is a bad psychological fit for Peterson. Still, he's the best publicly known suspect. Cooper sleuths eagerly await the updated edition of Peterson's autobiography for a possible departing confession (He is in his nineties now, but in decent health). Regardless, I think it's safe to say he's not Dan Cooper.

Mel Wilson

Ralph Himmelsbach, one of the principal investigators of the case, believes Cooper must have been someone with a criminal background. An "old con" looking for one last big score. Few serious Cooper suspects have had Himmelsbach's requisite profile. And only one, as far as anyone knows, has been missing since the hijacking. In 1971, just weeks before Norjak, Mel Wilson left his family home in Minnesota to travel to a sentencing hearing for a counterfeiting conviction. He disappeared forever. Despite going missing soon before the hijacking, he was never on the radar as a suspect in this case until one of his daughters started posting his story online sometime around when Larry Carr opened up the case. This makes him, along with Dick Lepsy, among the handful of serious suspects to come to light in the last ten years.

Wilson is a fascinating study, he was a man right out of the movies. Physically imposing, intelligent, charming, he was smooth-talker who was always working an angle. His preference was counterfeiting, and the descriptions available to us say he was very talented in his art. He was a classic confidence man. If you watch the Unsolved Mysteries episode on Wilson, you will find out he was also a ladies man. After he went missing, his family found out about another family he had also abandoned years before under very similar circumstances.

As for being a viable Cooper suspect, I'm skeptical but here's the case: Wilson was intelligent, a fugitive from justice who went missing right before the hijacking, he fits the physical description and he smoked and drank. His charm and personality seem to match Cooper's disarming persona. Wilson wore suits and he preferred loafers. Superficially, he looks like a decent candidate. It seems unlikely he could have planned this heist while in the middle of a legal battle, but it's possible.

The case against Wilson is based not on his inability to plan such a heist, nor whether he would commit such a crime. Instead, it's based simply on his lack of knowledge and skills. He did not have any previous parachuting experience, that we know about. Parachuting experience is not a prerequisite for a Cooper suspect, and the FBI now believes Cooper had very little knowledge about skydiving at all. (I believe the FBI is simply wrong, we know Cooper felt comfortable putting on a parachute harness, which is not normal and I invite any neophyte to try on a parachute harness without instruction.) Wilson also doesn't have any of the aviation knowledge Cooper apparently had. Finally, Wilson is yet another suspect who has no connection to the particle evidence found on Cooper's tie. (An effort was made by me to find companies in MN that worked with unalloyed titanium, but none could be found.)

What really makes me skeptical is the fact Wilson was a counterfeiter. Why would someone who prints his own money jump out of an airplane for $200,000? People stick to their habits, and I believe Wilson left his family for Las Vegas (or somewhere else) and continued his career printing money and running cons. Without an existing modus operandi there are a lot of logistical holes for an amateur like Wilson to fill. Dan Cooper was the first hijacker to leave an aircraft, had he been the second or third then perhaps Wilson could have been a possibility. Finally, if Cooper was a criminal known to law enforcement, it is my belief the FBI would have solved the case, regardless of whether he lived or died in the jump.

Still, there's no reason not to do a full vetting. Since so few serious suspects have come to light, there's certainly no harm in pursuing him. Especially considering Wilson fits the FBI view that Cooper was an amateur who died in the jump. It beggars belief that the FBI has refused to consider Wilson a suspect. One of Wilson's daughters spoke with the FBI and pursued this through multiple agencies, but got a tepid response, later receiving a letter stating "During any given investigation, the FBI receives many tips … In accordance with DOJ policy, we cannot discuss details of ongoing investigations. This includes not disclosing subjects considered and/or excluded, and investigative techniques that may be used … rest assured that the FBI pursues all leads that we believe will provide us with information of investigative value. I apologize that we are unable to disclose the nature and extent of our investigative response."

This letter was in response to a request to compare Wilson's DNA with the profiles from the tie. It was a request that came from the missing person case agent. It also meant that the woman looking for her father was not able to get a definitive answer on this question. I do not believe Mel Wilson is Dan Cooper, however, there is no reason not to have his DNA compared to the sample from the tie, or to check his fingerprints against those collected from the plane after the hijacking. Wilson's surviving family certainly deserve that much.

Kenny Christiansen

Christiansen has gotten an inordinate amount of press coverage, including an episode of Brad Meltzer's "Decoded", for being such a bad suspect. He even played a prominent role in Geoffrey Gray's indispensable "Skyjack". Kenny's brother, Lyle Christiansen, has been the primary source of speculation regarding his involvement in Norjak. The full profile on Kenny can be found in Robert Blevins' and Skipp Porteous' book "Into the Blast; The True Story of DB Cooper."

The bare-bones case is that Kenny, then a purser (lead flight attendant) for Northwest, planned Norjak with his friend "Bernie GeeMan" ("Bernie" is a living person and I choose not to name him). Kenny, a mild-mannered Midwesterner, was a former WWII paratrooper who had the prerequisite knowledge of the 727 and experience with the airlines and their operations. His partner, Bernie, was the wheel-man who would pick up Kenny once he reached the ground. GeeMan and Kenny's whereabouts during the hijacking are known only to them, as they were camping together at the time of the heist.

After the hijacking, the claim from Blevins et al. is Christiansen experienced a lifestyle change. He bought property and a house, loaned $5000 to GeeMan's sister, purchased expensive stamps and coins and otherwise lived a comfortable life after Norjak when before he was just scraping by. This paradigm shift, we're told, happened very soon after the Cooper hijacking. Porteous and Blevins have produced plentiful speculation and circumstantial evidence to feed their thesis. Among the more entertaining finds was the Decoded team discovering a framed-out box in the attic of Christiansen's old house; a place to hide money, they suggest.

It all makes for good theatre. And maybe more than that. Christiansen's aviation knowledge actually makes him a better suspect than some of the critics in the DB Cooper forums will admit. There are also some serious problems with the story. Physically, Kenny is too short. He has pale skin. In my opinion, he's only vaguely reminiscent of any of the Cooper sketches. Most importantly, the primary circumstantial claims from "Into the

Blast" about an unexpected surfeit of money right after the hijacking has been dismantled piecemeal over the last few years. Documents have come to light showing Kenny did not pay for his house in one lump sum of cash, but instead paid off a standard mortgage over many years.

Christiansen was a lifetime bachelor who did not have kids or anyone dependent upon him. He lived a simple, even boring, life. It's the sort of lifestyle financial planners would love. This leaves a lot of disposable income for other assets, like his coin and stamp collection; a piece of circumstantial evidence I find to be particularly specious. The value of Christiansen's stamp and coin collection has never been confirmed. Estimates have ranged from $30,000 to $400,000. Without a full catalogue, we can't know for sure. But even a six-figure collection would have been within reach of a lifetime bachelor who purchased gold and silver coins throughout the 1970's and 1980's, especially if the coins were appraised in the last ten years.

There are other problems. Obviously, there's the tie issue. Kenny would not have been exposed to pure titanium and some of the other metallic particles in his day-to-day life. Advocates who are cognizant of the tie evidence typically explain it away by suggesting Cooper's tie was purchased at a thrift store prior to the hijacking. Not in this case. Blevins and Porteous suggest in their "General Overview of the Case" that they can connect the tie tack to Christiansen. However, we know from Tom Kaye's study that the tie and tie tack were a mated pair. If Christiansen can't account for the particles on the tie, then he couldn't have owned it or the tie tack.

There are still more problems. Any Cooper story involving an accomplice is immediately suspect. Especially if the accomplice is said to have successfully rendezvoused with Cooper. Even Richard McCoy, who painstakingly ordered his hijacked plane along a very specific route and was able to land very close to his chosen landing zone, failed to meet up with his getaway driver (his wife). Cooper was very hands-off when it came to the flight path; he directed the plane to fly south to Mexico, with a gas stop in Reno. That's it. He never checked in with the cockpit for any information on the plane's heading or location. If Cooper had an accomplice, they were playing Hide and Seek.

Another wrinkle: Christiansen continued to fly for Northwest after the hijacking. It is very probable (though it hasn't been confirmed) he flew with at least one of the flight attendants from Norjak, who would have recognized him as the hijacker. Blevins and Porteous believe the fact Christiansen worked for Northwest was one of the primary reasons he was able to avoid detection. The FBI would never conceive of this hijacking as an inside job, their reasoning goes. Once again, we don't have access to the FBI files so we don't know for sure, but the FBI investigation was very thorough. It's unlikely they overlooked the possibility of a Northwest employee committing this hijacking. Besides, you can't escape the fact Christiansen could have encountered someone from the hijacking for years and years after the fact. It was a terrible risk to take.

Finally, this story leaves the Tena Bar money find completely in the air. Blevins and Porteous suggest the possibility of a plant. While I now believe the money found at Tena Bar got there through natural processes, I was once open to the possibility of a plant. No longer. There is actual video evidence from the original FBI excavation confirming reports of a significant debris field of money fragments, which precludes the possibility of a ruse. The money must have arrived on the banks of the Columbia only through natural processes. (There's an economic reason against a plant theory; $6,000 is simply too much money for a thief to throw away on a red herring. It would be about $30,000 in today's money.)

As with all of these suspects, we await the DNA from the missing cigarette butts to compare familial DNA from other members of the Christiansen family to completely eliminate Kenny from the suspect list. This is unlikely to ever happen. Still, we can fit suspects to the evidence and work from there. Christiansen has part of the background I would look for in a Cooper suspect, but he only fits part of the picture. Everything else, from his appearance to his life after the hijacking, points away from him being Dan Cooper.

Richard McCoy

McCoy is complicated, both as a person and as a suspect in Norjak. He was a Mormon Sunday school teacher, a family man with a wife and two kids, a decorated Vietnam combat veteran, he was studying to be a police officer at Brigham Young University. Four months after the Cooper hijacking, McCoy used a fake grenade and a handgun to hijack a United Airlines 727 and hold it for a $500,000 ransom. Sentenced to 45 years for the crime, McCoy escaped from a federal prison and died a few months later in a shootout with FBI agents.

You can get the entire rundown on Richard McCoy's life before and after his hijacking in the book "DB Cooper; The Real McCoy" by Bernie Rhodes. Be forewarned, it is one the more difficult-to-read books related to this case. It has long passages of boring, sometimes incomprehensible jargon interrupted by short spurts of interesting details of FBI and law enforcement processes and politics. Nothing is presented in a logical order and I personally found much of the book a struggle to read. Rhodes exaggerates his claims to make the connection between Cooper and McCoy stronger; sometimes it appears as though he fabricates evidence. It is my opinion that most of the connections outlined in the book connecting Cooper and McCoy are coincidence.

With that resounding endorsement, let's look at the connections the book makes between the two hijackings: McCoy and Cooper both used pre-written notes (Cooper used one, McCoy used many), they both sat in the back row of their 727s on the same side of the aircraft. They both directed refueling trucks to nearly the same position outside of the aircraft. They both left a clip-on tie (!) on the aircraft after exiting. Those are the major connections, Rhodes suggests there are over twenty total connections between McCoy to Cooper. Most of these connections are very weak. Cooper and McCoy committed the same crime, hijacking a 727 with the intention of jumping out the back, so of course many of their methods would be similar.

It's not necessary to go in and examine every connection between Cooper and McCoy. The reality is McCoy was a copycat and there are enough differences to prove McCoy and Cooper are not the same person. When McCoy was originally apprehended, we know his picture was shown to several of the Norjak eyewitnesses and they did not identify him as Cooper. McCoy also had a much different personality than Cooper. McCoy was forceful and rude when dealing the crew, and he was much quicker to anger. McCoy wore a disguise, which Cooper did not do. McCoy used a fake grenade and a handgun to hijack his aircraft, while Cooper used a homemade bomb-looking device; more, Cooper spun a yarn about the device being electronic and even told the cockpit crew to be judicious with their radio communications because it might cause an accidental detonation and destroy the airplane. McCoy made no such suggestion.

McCoy and Cooper were very different people. McCoy was uncomfortable in his own skin, using heavy makeup and a wig to disguise his appearance. He dressed in loud colors, a blue tie, a red and blue striped jacket, and a green shirt with flowers on it. Cooper dressed normally, in much more subdued colors. McCoy's notes were verbose compared to the concise orders Cooper gave his cockpit crew. Cooper was quite calm, even charming, throughout the hijacking. No one would describe McCoy's crime in such a way. McCoy brought skydiver gear, including a jumpsuit and helmet. Cooper did not.

The tie is the final piece of evidence that absolutely eliminates McCoy. Bernie Rhodes believes the tie belonged to McCoy and that members of McCoy's family recognized the tie as belonging to him. This can not be true. Firstly, we know McCoy didn't work with titanium, like most of the suspects we've looked at. However, McCoy also didn't smoke. Tom Kaye found that Cooper's tie was saturated with particles associated with smoking. It had more material on it than a similar tie from the same era Kaye tested, meaning the tie was worn very often by a smoker. I inherited my grandfather's extensive collection of ties, and a quick look under a blacklight showed none of the particle density found by Kaye using the same method on Cooper's tie. My grandfather was a non-smoker like McCoy, who also had to wear a tie every day to work for his entire life. The lack of visible particles is, to me, quite telling. If the tie found on the plane belonged to Dan Cooper, then

Richard McCoy can't be our mysterious hijacker.

Don Burnworth

This is one of the most entertaining sagas of the Cooper world. If I were to write a screenplay using the Cooper hijacking as a template, I would take all the elements from Burnworth's story and use them in the movie. There are mobsters, kidnappings, betrayals, and flights from justice. I simply can't do it justice here because I'm limiting myself to "the important stuff", the actual facts of the Cooper case. A complete narrative is available in Bruce Smith's book.

Burnworth was a United Airlines captain around the time of the hijacking who got caught up in a wild divorce and some other legal troubles. Basically, his wife took custody of the kids, and he decided to take the children out of the country to protect them from his ex-wife's abusive boyfriend. That sort of action, even when justified, can get you into serious trouble. Eventually, Burnworth was forced to return to the United States where he was arrested and questioned about not only his daughters and ex-wife, but also about the DB Cooper hijacking.

He spent some time in jail, but eventually he was able to clear up all the legal questions surrounding his divorce. Long story short, his children returned to the United States from Burnworth's hideaway in Germany. During this time, Burnworth was fired from his job at UAL. He was able to get it back after an intervention from the National Labor Relations Board. Things improved from there, and Burnworth remained a United Airlines captain until his retirement.

Some people consider him to be a good match to the Cooper sketch. I don't see it; Burnworth had a large and crooked nose that is lacking from the Cooper descriptions and sketch. He does match the physical description, and being a 727 pilot at the time of the hijacking he would have had the knowledge Cooper appeared to have about the aircraft, and he otherwise would have been capable of pulling off this heist.

The problem is, like so many pilots, he had zero interest in ever leaving a functional aircraft and relying on some flimsy parachute. He had a decent job that he enjoyed at UAL, which removes his motive. He wasn't working with unalloyed titanium. He was investigated by the FBI, presumably his picture was shown to Flo and Tina and Mitchell to no avail. It's a fascinating story, but there's no "here" here. Burnworth is not our hijacker.

Robert Wesley Rackstraw

Everyone knows "that guy." That guy who always tells a big whopper of a story. That guy who's always bragging about what he's done. That guy who HAS to be lying about winning the four gold medals at the Sarajevo Olympics. But part of you believes That Guy. Some of his stories are true... He has an old picture of himself with Richard Nixon. He has a scar from a bear attack. And what about his friend from the motorcycle gang? Rackstraw is That Guy. Thomas Colbert (TJC) believes Rackstraw is DB Cooper. (Most of the information found here is from TJC's website and book.) Rackstraw is a living person, but after his love affair with the media in the late 1970's during his murder trial, and the subsequent History Channel special about him 2016, make him a public figure in my estimation. So let's get to the story...

Rackstraw went into the army in the 1960's, attending the infantry jump school at Fort Benning in 1967. In 1969, he becomes both a fixed-wing and helicopter pilot. Rackstraw serves in Vietnam. According to TJC, who is himself a crime television guru and author, Rackstraw does some freelance work for the CIA while in southeast Asia. When Rackstraw returns stateside, he gets embroiled in a messy divorce. The Army decides to look into Rackstraw's background after he's accused of domestic assault; they find that Lt. Rackstraw lied about his college credentials, and lied about his rank and military decorations. He is forced to resign from the military.

From Alabama, Rackstraw heads to the Pacific Northwest where he works as a charter pilot for realtors who need aerial photographs. He spends a lot of time in the area, up to and after the Cooper hijacking. He eventually ends up working for a floor and deck laying company in San Francisco. Rackstraw's career in crime begins in earnest at this time. He will often wear a suit and tie around shipyards, looking like a supervisor or office worker. This allows him to steal valuables with impunity. Sometime during this period, Rackstraw meets longtime confidant Dick Briggs (who later became a drug dealer in the late 70s). By the mid-1970's, Rackstraw was on law enforcement's radar. He was implicated in the theft of military weapons and explosives; check-kiting, ramming his vehicle through a business competitor's building, stealing goods, stealing dynamite and murdering his stepfather... Among other crimes. He goes on trial for murder in July of 1978. Rackstraw shows up in a wheelchair, claiming to be a disabled veteran of five Vietnam campaigns as a Green Beret captain. His actual service record doesn't show up until after the trial. He is found "Not Guilty."

In October of 1978, still looking at criminal charges for his other hobbies, Rackstraw fakes his own death. Sending a bogus "Mayday" call over the radio, Rackstraw claims to ditch into the sea near Monterey Bay. Rackstraw is eventually found and arrested by police in January of 1979. He spends the next year in jail before being released. Law enforcement clears him of being DB Cooper at this time. He stays out of trouble, and out of the media spotlight, for the next seventeen years. He becomes a college instructor with degrees in economics and law, before getting into trouble again. This time around the charges are mundane, DUI and resisting arrest. The public becomes familiar with Rackstraw again in 2016, when he is prominently featured as a Cooper suspect in a History Channel special on Norjak.

Why is Rackstraw a Cooper suspect? For one thing, he claimed to be our mysterious hijacker on at least one occasion while he was in jail. He abandoned his confession almost immediately, probably when he found out he could still be charged with the hijacking. There are other reasons too, Rackstraw lived in the Pacific Northwest, knew the area from his job as a pilot, and his whereabouts during the hijacking are unknown. Rackstraw has the skills Cooper needed. He went through jump school and would have been quite comfortable with parachuting gear. He may have learned in Vietnam that the 727 was being used as jump platform for secret missions being done by the CIA. He has the criminal background Ralph Himmelsbach was looking for. (Though Rackstraw's career would have been the reverse of what we'd expect: he would have started with the big heist, then moved on to smaller thefts and cons before working his way back up to murder.) Rackstraw even has a relative named "Ed Cooper" who might have inspired the Dan Cooper alias.

There's always a catch, however. Rackstraw would have been in his late 20's at the time of the hijacking. Some reports on Cooper put him as old as 60, but most witnesses put the hijacker in his mid to late forties. Rackstraw doesn't have the swarthy complexion Cooper is reported to have. Tina Mucklow, the stewardess who spent the most time with Cooper, did not think Rackstraw was the hijacker when she was shown his picture and video on the History Channel special. In TJC's book, we find out Rachstraw lacked empathy (there's a chilling account of him pointing and shooting a BB gun at his step sister), whereas DB Cooper tried to tip the stewardesses and he ordered meals for the crew. This is the thoughtful empathy Rackstraw, as portrayed by TJC, completely lacked.

 The biggest hurdle in connecting Rackstraw with Cooper remains the Tena Bar money find. TJC claims Rackstraw had his friend Briggs give the money to Dwayne Ingram to "find" on Tena Bar, thus throwing the feds off his trail. There are a number of problems with this theory, chief among them the fact the money had obviously been exposed to the elements long enough to alter the bills substantially. They had clumped together into a single, solid mass and the rubber bands attached to the bills crumbled away when touched. There was a field of money shards found up and down the bar, and there is video of FBI agents unearthing fragments of money at least a foot deep into the sand. There is simply no possibility the money was planted there in the late 1970's as Colbert claims.

 When you're looking for DB Cooper suspects, a military-trained con man with the gift of gab and a long history of stunning crimes is a good place to go looking. But you can't ignore the fact he was investigated by law enforcement and cleared of the hijacking. He never worked in an industry that used pure titanium and none of the main witnesses in the case identify him as Dan Cooper. However much Rackstraw may be "That Guy," he's not our guy. He's not our hijacker.

LD Cooper

The story of LD Cooper exploded on the media like a fireworks show and disappeared just as quickly. Media fawned over Marla Cooper, a photogenic forty-something, when she announced that her uncle Lynn Doyle Cooper was the real DB Cooper. Rumors persisted that her story was so convincing the FBI might even close the book on Dan Cooper. LD was the "most promising" suspect ever in the case. Details were difficult to come by until recently when Marla published a book about her uncle's connections to Norjak.[41]

Lynn Doyle Cooper was a surveyor in Washington state who served in the Korean War. His brother once worked for Boeing and might have picked up knowledge about the 727 there. Marla claimed the two conspired to commit the hijacking, using handheld radios to meet up after LD jumped out of N467US. Marla further remembers seeing her two uncles on Thanksgiving Day in 1971. The two arrived in a car; LD was badly hurt and covered in blood. Marla stated her two uncles later went to the home of a fourth brother who took the two in. One of Marla's cousins later confirmed LD was badly hurt. In the days and weeks after the hijacking, her uncles scoured the woods searching for the lost money, but never found a single twenty. The Radio ended up in the junk drawer, and the whole episode was lost to time. At least until Marla's father talked about the events just before he died, rekindling the whole affair.

---

[41]The book is called "DB's Niece (In the Raw, Unedited!): The story of my hijacked life! (The Memoirs of Marla Wynn Cooper Book 1)" by Marla Cooper. I found the book particularly difficult to read, interesting tidbits about what it's like dealing with the FBI are hidden in long passages of childhood reminiscences that have nothing to do with the Cooper case. Besides passing a lie detector, very little evidence is presented in the book to defend its thesis.

Marla brought her story to the attention to the FBI and SA Curtis Eng.[42] This is where the story gets interesting. Eng is infamous for being an unemotive and impatient statue when dealing with people and their crazy DB Cooper theories. Something about Marla's story caught his attention. When Marla talked about how her uncle had lost the money in the jump, Eng got very excited. Apparently Eng was sick of hearing stories about genius Cooper suspects planting money on Tena Bar to fool those meatheads at the FBI. So Eng pursued the matter, giving Marla an extensive polygraph exam, which she passed. The FBI later tested DNA and looked for LD's fingerprints to check against the evidence collected from the airplane at Reno. The DNA produced no match, the fingerprint analysis came up with nothing, and no physical link was ever made between LD and Norjak.

Taken at face value, the story is interesting but it's no more compelling than any of the other stories about Cooper suspects from people like Jo Weber. The forty-year-old memories of a then eight-year-old girl about her uncle being hurt on Thanksgiving day ain't exactly what I'd call... promising... It's actually pretty thin. We can take all of Marla's memories as Gospel truth, and it still doesn't warrant the investment Eng made. Other than Marla's recollections of the night she saw her uncle LD badly injured, she makes zero connections to Norjak.

Why isn't LD Cooper DB Cooper? First, LD Cooper's military record did not include any parachute training that we know of, and LD Cooper otherwise had no experience parachuting or skydiving. Marla suggests LD's military records are incomplete, or fabricated. Regardless, no one can put LD in a parachute harness.

---

[42] It's quite a mystery why the stoic Curtis Eng became so enamored with this particular story, especially considering the complete lack of evidence. Marla Cooper would go on to garner a lot of media attention, only to later see the FBI investigation come back negative. It represents another embarassing misstep for the FBI regarding this case.

Some of LD's DNA was tested against the tie, and no match was found (from Marla's book, it sounds like they tested LD's daughter and mother; having the mother tested would allow them to look only at LD's DNA). At least one fingerprint of LD's was tested against the samples taken from the aircraft, again to no success.

And of course, LD did not work with titanium. Nor did his brother, who Marla claims loaned the tie to LD. Marla even produced a photograph of her uncle wearing a skinny black tie with a tie tack that looks like the tie tack from DB Cooper's tie. But, the tie tack looks like it was inserted from the right (opposite of DB Cooper) and the photo is from 1964. The tie was available in 1964, but according to Marla her uncles were all blue collar guys who didn't wear ties very often. Funerals and weddings, basically. None of them would have been wearing the tie often enough (or any tie often enough) to put the density of particles Kaye found on DB Cooper's tie.

Once again, for the story to work the tie must have been purchased at a thrift store, sometime very soon before the hijacking. Just like all the other suspects. There are more problems. The Cooper brothers were all hard-drinking men, borderline alcoholics. I doubt, based on Marla's description of their behavior, that any of them could hijack an aircraft and not drink. DB Cooper ordered one drink, and spilled about half of it. One drink, over six hours. Not the behavior one would expect from a heavy drinker.

Eng is quoted by Marla as saying LD had "the background for this hijacking." Which is odd, since LD didn't have any first-hand knowledge of aviation. It's possible his brother Dewey, who worked at Boeing on the 727s, might have known about the rear-stairs being a good skydiving platform, or about the indent-flap settings. But overall, the stuff DB Cooper knew about the 727 exceeded what we'd expect LD Cooper to know.

Marla is adamant about her recollections, but they are the recollections of an eight-year-old girl. I'm sure her uncle LD was hurt at some point (my guess would be a DUI-related car accident) and at some point was being driven around by her other uncle. I wouldn't be shocked if they did search for Cooper and his money. But nothing about her story matches the description of DB Cooper as an "executive type" patiently waiting for hours to jump out of an airplane, sipping a single order of bourbon.

Minor Suspect Profiles

John List

Some may remember List as the man who murdered his entire family in order to guarantee their place in Heaven and disappeared for almost 18 years before America's Most Wanted caught him using an age-progressed model of his face. He was also considered a Cooper suspect since he matched the description and disappeared two weeks before the hijacking. However, he already had $200,000 from draining his family's bank accounts, he didn't need to steal more money. Certainly not right away. Further, his career as an accountant doesn't match the particles found on the Cooper tie, List does not have any kind of parachuting background and he did not otherwise have the knowledge or skills to pull off this heist. At least, not under such a tight schedule. After his capture, he readily admitted to the murders of his family, but denied being the hijacker.

Ted Mayfield

Mayfield is well-known in the Cooper saga. A skydiver and pilot who had several run-ins with the law, fingers pointed to him almost immediately after Norjak. He was even acquainted with Ralph Himmelsbach before the hijacking. Mayfield certainly had the skills and probably the moxie to pull off such a stunt. However, Mayfield contacted the FBI on the evening of the hijacking, only a few hours after Cooper jumped from the plane. It would have been very difficult for even a competitive skydiver like Mayfield to cover his tracks so quickly. Most importantly, Mayfield is known to be of very short stature, about 5'3" and thus he does not fit the description of the hijacker.

Jack Coffelt

A conman who spent most of his life in prison, Coffelt claimed he was Cooper in 1972. Apparently the goal was to make money out of a movie deal, but Coffelt himself died in 1975. The FBI interviewed him, but his story was wrong on several important details (which they have never released). Regardless, the details of Coffelt's story we do know about are completely wrong. He claimed to have landed near Mt. Hood, which was too far south and too far east. He also claimed to have an accomplice and that, even though he landed very far from the Victor 23 corridor, they somehow met up and made their escape. The story is still being sold to the public by one of Coffelt's former cellmates.

Barb Dayton

Perhaps the most interesting story in the Cooper Saga, Barbara Dayton was a middle-aged woman who worked as a university librarian. She was also a pilot and mechanic who owned and worked on small aircraft at Thun Airfield in Washington. Originally born Robert Dayton, she received Washington State's first sex-change operation in the late 1960's. A natural storyteller, she spun a complex yarn to her small circle of pilot friends about switching back to her male persona to commit the Cooper hijacking. Using the lights of Portland to time her jump, Barbara claimed to land well south of the Columbia River, hiding the money in a cistern... At some point moving the money to Tena Bar in time for Brian Ingram to find some of it in 1980. While Bobby Dayton does bear a resemblance to Dan Cooper, Barb was too short, her landing zone was too far south of Portland and her explanation for the Tena Bar find is at odds with the available science. Ron and Pat Forman's book "The Legend of DB Cooper: Death by Natural Causes" presents Barbara's full story.

John Lake

The Sports Editor at Newsweek, Lake disappeared on December 10, 1967, somewhere between Midtown and Greenwich Village in NYC. He has never been seen again. The only reason I'm writing about him here is because a Cooper forum member mentioned Lake while listing all the possible Cooper suspects from the NamUs missing person database. Lake is about the right age, and bears a passing resemblance to the sketch. (Something that becomes annoyingly clear to anyone investigating the Cooper case is just how many people there are who bear a likeness to one of the FBI sketches.) Lake can be immediately eliminated because he had no knowledge of parachuting, aviation, the Pacific Northwest, nor would we expect to find unalloyed titanium on his tie. In all likelihood, Lake met with foul play on his walk home and his body was never recovered from the Hudson River. His disappearance is an interesting mystery itself and more information can be found at johnlake.com. I use Lake as a control for other suspects, if a candidate is not a better fit for Cooper than he, I disregard their story straightaway.

Jack Collins

Profiled in the book "My Father was D.B. Cooper", Jack Collins was a pilot, skydiver and an insurance agent with money troubles who was always looking for a get-rich-quick scheme. Collins actually used his skydiving hobby to fake injuries for insurance claims. His brother was a 727 pilot, and according to Jack Collins' son, the two perpetrated the Norjak heist to help provide for Jack's struggling family. Unfortunately, any theory involving an accomplice is extremely suspect; Richard McCoy, who hijacked a plane several months after DB Cooper, had to constantly communicate with the cockpit in order to align the aircraft with his dropzone. Even then, McCoy failed to meet up with his ride. Cooper made no attempt to find out the plane's location from the cockpit, and there's no evidence Cooper had a specific landing zone in mind. Still, John and his brother had the requisite knowledge of the 727 and of skydiving to be plausible suspects. However, once again, we find someone who does not fit with Kaye's tie findings. Unless something other than weak circumstantial evidence emerges, we can safely eliminate Collins as a suspect. (Note: Duane Weber used "John C Collins" as an alias, and even served time under that name.)

William Wolfgang Gossett

A military man with parachuting experience, Gossett supposedly confessed to the hijacking to friends and relatives in the 90's. Gossett is an interesting suspect. He had the military parachuting background many believe Cooper had, and he matched the physical description. Gossett also lived in the Pacific Northwest before the hijacking and would have had the local knowledge Cooper showed. Most interesting, Gossett served overseas when the Dan Cooper comic book was available, and Gossett could read and speak French. At the time of the hijacking, Gossett lived and worked in Utah, giving him a very narrow time window to travel to and from the Pacific Northwest. Gossett claimed to have the Cooper ransom money in a safe deposit box. However, none of it has ever surfaced. It's another case of "he must have planted the money on Tena Bar" and that basically eliminates Gossett. The tie evidence also rules him out.

Ted Braden

Prior to Cooper's hijacking, few people knew that a 727 could be successfully jumped by a properly motivated skydiver. It's important to understand other airliners had rear stairs like the 727, but those planes had locking mechanisms on the stairs; the 727 did not. Second, it was not known whether opening the stairs during flight would make the aircraft dangerously unstable. During the hijacking, Boeing was actually contacted to address these and other concerns, and they had to reveal that yes, in fact, the airplane could be safely flown with the stairs down. Other than a few engineers at Boeing, the only people who knew the 727 was a serviceable jump platform were CIA and Special Forces operatives serving in Vietnam. Of those people, the best candidate to come to light has been Ted Braden, a special forces veteran with a capricious personality. He had the knowledge and the abilities to do this hijacking, but he was too short, standing at 5'8" tall. And once again, the tie evidence excludes him.

Additional Materials

Larry Carr's Profile

In 2007, then Norjack case agent Larry Carr joined the DropZone DB Cooper forum as "ckret" and posted a profile of who he thought DB Cooper was based on the FBI files and investigation to that point. He challenged the forum members to find a candidate who fit his profile. Many of the Cooper sleuths on the current DB Cooper forum believe we don't have any suspects who fit this profile. However, I believe "Dan LeClair," as presented in Gunther's book, is a good fit.

In bold italics is Larry Carr's profile as it was posted in 2007 on the DZ forum. My responses, based on Gunther's book, are in this book's standard font.

...who was DB Cooper?

-DB Cooper was not a drinker, he only had one drink and spilled a portion of that. If someone was a drinker, in a situation like this he would have had more than just one in the five hours he was on the plane.

Dan LeClair did drink socially, but there's nothing in his background to suggest he abused alcohol. After he left his family for life on the road, LeClair actually becomes disillusioned with his new underclass companions, who were mostly bar hounds (Gunther, p 118). As for the hijacking itself, LeClair did not drink specifically for the purpose of avoiding inopportune trips to the lavatory.

-He was not a chain smoker, he was on the aircraft for five hours and only smoked 8 cigarettes. That would make him a smoker of less than a pack-a-day and this under normal conditions.

The book doesn't mention LeClair's smoking habits in any detail, if at all. LeClair is certainly not described as a chain smoker, which would have been an easy detail to add if Gunther was creating a character, rather than reporting on a real individual. As an author myself, I like having characters who smoke, since it gives them something to do during breaks in the story. Regardless, smoking was so common for men during this era that it would not have been seen as an important detail.

-He spoke in an intelligent manner and never lost his cool, he was always polite throughout the ordeal.

This is so close to the man written about in Gunther's book that Carr could be summarizing the description of Dan LeClair from it. LeClair is described in the book as a college-educated sales executive, soft spoken and thoughtful (Gunther p 26).

-He had brown eyes (Schaffner saw his eyes before he put on the glasses, he looked directly at her several times urging her to read the note)

I hesitate to make any claims about what LeClair looked like physically. We have nothing more than Clara's description to go by and she never produced a photograph for analysis. (She did this for two very good reasons: she didn't want the FBI going after her or LeClair's family). The description we do get from Clara, as relayed by Gunther, are that LeClair's eyes were "piercing dark eyes that looked almost black" (p 24).

-He is 5'10 to 6'1 (Mucklow is 5'8 and spent 5 hours with Cooper, she would know if he was her height or taller. Have someone 5'8 stand next to someone 6 feet, the difference is obvious. Better yet, position yourself at a level of 5'8 and look at someone at a 6' elevation. Now spend 5 hours with that person, you'll know the difference. No one put Cooper under 5'10.

Same caveat here about LeClair's physical description. LeClair is described as being around six feet tall.

-He had olive skin (no make-up, neither Mucklow,

Schaffner or Hancock made comment on make-up which would have been very obvious. Again, do the math, put dark makeup on someone then sit next to them with your shoulders touching, you can see the make-up.)

Ditto the previous caveat, LeClair is described as having a complexion that turns to the color of "walnut wood" when tan (p 84). LeClair is a regular outdoorsmen, preferring to spend his free time on long hikes through the woods of the northwest. He had also worked occasionally as an agricultural laborer in the year before the hijacking.

-He had dark hair, receding with sideburns (no wig, this would have been painfully obvious, if a man was wearing a wig with a receding hair line and side burns everyone would have noticed, especially Mucklow and Schaffner.)

Ditto the caveat, LeClair is described as looking a little like "Ben Gazzara" (p 59).

-He was med built (no one put him over 190 lbs, in fact most put him 180 or under. Find a man 6 foot 180 lbs, thats a med to thin build.)

Ditto, LeClair is described as having a long and lean build (p 24).

These are the facts on his physical make-up, if your suspect does not match these you may want to start looking at someone else.

DB Cooper had A.D.D, his attention to detail was poor. He got the big picture, but missed the brush strokes. He was also a "know-it-all." The type of person who would learn a few facts and then become an expert on the subject. One of those people who has just enough knowledge to be dangerous.

This is another close match to Dan LeClair. At one point, Clara asked him how he got into Industrial Chemicals and his reply was "Oh, I read up on it." (p 89). The profile of LeClair is as an ultra-handyman, as comfortable doing mechanical repairs as he was jet-setting across the country in a suit to make a major sale.

DB Cooper most likely served in the military and upon leaving used his technical training as a contractor in the airline industry, in and around Seattle. He rose to a mid-level management position but when he could rise no further or his project never got off the ground, he quit or was fired, "because no one understood him or were just to stupid to get it."

LeClair did serve in the military. He used the GI bill to get a college education, and got into business as a salesman, and did indeed work his way up to middle management. This isn't a perfect match, but it's close. Carr did this profile before Kaye's work on the tie was completed, so Carr did not know about the titanium particles. Thanks to Kaye's work, we know Cooper most likely worked in industrial chemicals. Carr's guess about Cooper working in aviation is probably wrong.

Soon thereafter he ran into big financial problems that had a set deadline for resolution. Just as always he developed the "big picture" for getting the money but the escape was very poorly planned.

LeClair's financial problems were a product of his new life on the road. From reading the text, it's obvious the grind of making a living under the table as a transient worker weighed heavily on him. The book describes, over several chapters, his elation at his new-found freedom from an unhappy life and marriage, which is later balanced by his frustration with trying to make a life for himself on the run. As an intelligent man accustomed to a middle-class existence, struggling to get money for housing and meals must have been quite a shock.

And the escape? Perhaps Carr is right again. LeClair expected to walk out of his landing zone like someone on an afternoon hike. He lived in the Portland area and was a regular hiker, so he would have been comfortable with a 15-20 mile walk, even through rough terrain. Given a full day to do it, such a hike was within his abilities. However, his injury upon landing prevented this and caused him to ask for help, which is how he met with Clara.

Gunther Connections Annotated

Max Gunther's book "D.B. Cooper; What Really Happened" is out of print. Copies are quite affordable, but if the reader is not inclined to seek one out I have duplicated here the most important passages dealing with Dan LeClair's employment history before the hijacking and how he disappeared from his former life by wearing his everyday business attire.

Cooper worked in industrial chemicals (p 89):

> He (LeClair) was hired as a sales trainee in a New York-area company that manufactured industrial chemicals. As he explained to Clara, "It wasn't really selling. I was a salesman, the way somebody behind the counter in a store is a salesman, that's all." The job principally involved supervising and expediting customers' orders.
>
> ...
>
> "I asked him," Clara says, "how come he went to work for a chemicals company when he'd never taken a chemistry course in his life. I mean, how did he learn what he needed to know about the stuff his company made? You know what his answer was? He said, 'Oh, I read up on it.'"

LeClair worked his way up the ladder in the chemicals industry, being eventually promoted to management positions (p 97):

The decade of the 1960's had been a time of increasing trouble for Dan LeClair. In the 1950s his company had promoted him into jobs of progressively greater management responsibility, but in the 1960s he became ever more keenly aware that he really didn't want the responsibility, the pressure, or even the pay.

LeClair lost his job and was forced to work for another chemicals company, then another after that (p 98-99):

> A crisis occurred at work. ... The mistake was blamed on Dan LeClair. Perhaps he deserved the blame, and perhaps, as he protested, he did not. ... He lost his job.
>
> He found another sales job with a smaller chemicals company, but his luck had run out. The company was in trouble. The trouble abruptly grew worse after he was hired, and in a very short time the company turned belly-up.
>
> ...
>
> He managed to find a job of lesser pay and prestige at a still smaller company. This company, too, found life a struggle. Dan did not know how long his job would last, but he did not care very much.

LeClair leaving with his business suit:
> He told Lucy [pseudonym for his wife at the time] he was going on a business trip, and on the morning of his planned departure he arrived at work, said he was sick and was going back home. By this double ruse he hoped to gain a few days' head start before any kind of hunt got organized.

He took the suitcase of stored clothes to a railroad station. In the men's room he changed into casual clothes and put his business suit, shirt, tie, and shoes in the suitcase. He caught a train to Washington, DC.

LeClair wore glasses (p 24):

> If she had to pick a known face for comparison, she says, she would say he bore a distant resemblance to actor Ben Gazzara. He had dark hair and piercing dark eyes that looked almost black. He wore glasses. He appeared to be in his middle forties. His body was long and lean.

At least one eyewitness believed Cooper's sunglasses were prescription.

LeClair removed his glasses to change his appearance (p 113):

> [Dan LeClair] made only the barest attempt to change the look of his face. The only item of facial disguise Clara knows of is that he kept his glasses in his pocket for a time. He could see tolerably well without them.

LeClair uses cash to purchase an item, but he doesn't use a twenty (we know Dan Cooper (p 58):

> She stopped to buy groceries, and at [Dan's] request and with his money---but not a twenty-dollar bill, she recalls---she bought a bottle of brandy.

Cooper received about $19 in change when he ordered his drink.

Dan LeClair avoids plane travel after leaving his wife; he was worried about being identified. This suggests he was a regular flier before absconding (p 113):

> Throughout his wanderings until the final great adventure, [Dan LeClair] would studiously avoid airlines. He stuck to short-haul trains and buses, partly because they are cheaper than air travel but mainly because their passengers are anonymous. Nobody asks who you are when you buy a ticket for a short bus ride. Nor is there a flight attendant patrolling the aisle, looking at the passengers' faces.

Gunther's interaction with Seattle Office Special Agent J. Earl Milnes (p 63):

> Milnes' witnesses recalled that the hijacker had worn a brown suit, or perhaps it was gray. His tie was blue, red, brown, or some other color. He was wearing tinted glasses, or perhaps they weren't tinted, or maybe he wasn't wearing glasses at all, come to think of it. He was either lean or husky, and he weighed 175 pounds, or 200, or 225, or something. His hair was black or brown, and perhaps he was partly bald.

This passage is particularly interesting since we now know the FBI had the tie from the very beginning. Maybe the description of the tie varied from the eyewitnesses, but the FBI knew exactly what it looked like. To me, this is clearly an attempt by Milnes to "fact check" Gunther's story. Unfortunately, Clara would never have seen the tie, nor did she ever claim to have seen the tie.

Description of LeClair's clothing (p 138):

Now that he had procrastinated for months, he had given himself more opportunity to save some money. Perhaps he bought the suit at a pawn shop. At any rate, he obtained a light, warm suit in a dark russet material. Clara never saw the jacket but recalls that the pants fitted him somewhat baggily but tolerably well.

Passenger Mitchell described him as being unfashionably dressed. Passenger Robert Gregory described Cooper's jacket as "russet-colored" in interviews after the hijacking.

Original Parachute Paper

I wrote this paper to answer what I believed was the erroneous suggestion that Cooper had little chance of surviving his jump. As noted earlier in the book, I have since revised my initial conclusions. I believe it is even more unlikely that Cooper failed to pull his ripcord than the following paper suggests, but this paper nicely outlines the issue.

Survival Probability Analysis of the D.B. Cooper Hijacking using Historical Parachuting Data

December 1, 2014
Martin Andrade Jr, MBA

Abstract

The D.B. Cooper hijacking is the only unsolved air piracy case in U.S. history. Understanding the true probability of Cooper surviving the jump out of Northwest Orient's 727 is a key obstacle in understanding both who Cooper was and what happened after the crew lost contact with him. By comparing the jump to similar bailout situations during WWII by RAF bomber crews, an approximate survival probability of at least 80% is found. An analysis of the drop zone as it pertains to Cooper's survival is included, and the Tena Bar money find is discussed in regards to this new understanding of the jump.

Introduction

On November 24th, 1971, a man calling himself Dan Cooper jumped out of the back of a Northwest Orient Airlines 727 with $200,000 strapped to his body, never to be seen or heard from again. Interviews with thousands of suspects, over four decades of searching by the FBI and others, in one of the largest and most expensive manhunts in history, has resulted in nothing conclusive about Cooper's identity or fate. Most of the lead FBI agents in the case believe Cooper died in the jump [1].

Without hard evidence such as a body, the assessment of the survivability of Cooper's jump has been left to skydiving experts, drawing from their personal experiences alone [2]. This is problematic for a number of reasons, including a lack of access to their experiences and an inability to measure their biases created by their training and experience. Instead, an independent analysis done using the largest available dataset of inexperienced jumpers available will bypass any biases. There is such a dataset, thousands of aircrews were forced to bail out of their damaged planes during World War Two.

The Jump

Skydivers in the United States experience a fatality in every 150,000 jumps. Main canopy failures happen approximately once in every 750 openings [3]. This an exceptional safety record produced by diligence and regulation. Equipment is carefully maintained and packed, jumps are generally done under controlled conditions and in good weather. There are numerous safety regulations in place, and skydiving businesses have an obvious incentive to make every jump done at their drop zones as safe as possible. These were definitely not the conditions under which Dan Cooper jumped.

Instead, Cooper faced a range of more challenging circumstances. He jumped at night, in cold weather with high winds, rain, limited visibility, without a working reserve parachute and laden down with a bulky canvas sack of money tied to his waist or to his parachute harness [4]. His level of parachuting experience is unknown, but the ease with which he was seen putting on the NB6 parachute he chose suggests he had some training, most likely from the military [5]. It is unknown if Cooper had any jumping experience beyond this, so the following analysis assumes he only had the most basic military training, which is congruent with the evidence.

During WWII tens of thousands of airmen had to bail out of damaged aircraft under difficult conditions, without reserve parachutes, using equipment they did not pack or maintain themselves, in cold weather, with little training and no prior practice jumps, and not under the supervision of experienced jumpers. In particular, the RAF Bomber Command (RAFBC), operating almost exclusively at night, will give the closest analogy for the survivability of Cooper's jump.

From the broadest perspective, approximately 25% of RAF Bomber Command airmen shot down during the war were captured or successfully evaded [6]. This gives us our minimum boundary. Cooper's survival chances are no lower than 1 in 4. However, many RAFBC casualties were from training missions, and their crews generally never wore their emergency parachutes. British bombers had very small emergency hatches, which often hindered crewmen trying to bail out. Another problem of bomber design made it especially difficult for pilots to get out of their aircraft, resulting in pilots staying with their aircraft all the way down to ground impact [7]. Many crew were killed and wounded by bullets and ack ack and never jumped. Taken together, we can assume Cooper's survival chances were much higher than this 25% number.

How much higher? An example of a typical bailout situation, described by a surviving Mid-Upper Gunner [8] in a RAF Lancaster bomber, involved the pilot staying with the aircraft, the crew scrambling for parachutes, six of seven crewman bailing out at 4500 feet above the ground, and five of the six finding themselves alive on the ground. The canopy opening was described as painful, and the landing caused injury to the mid-upper gunner, but he was still able to walk away and seek refuge. This was one of over a dozen RAF nighttime bailout scenarios collected for this paper. In total, thirty-four survivors were found for forty-three reported bailouts, a 79.1% survival rate [9].

Because they flew at night, there are very few firsthand RAF accounts that are useful, so getting a bigger sample size will require more complicated calculus. Since we know the approximate bailout rates for bomber crews [See note 9], we can test the bailout rate against survivors on the ground and get an estimate for the survivability of these wartime combat jumps. Then, especially in the case of American bombers, we can test these estimates against actual eyewitness reports.

The 91st Bombardment Group will be used in this first test

[10]. American daylight bombers had a 50% bailout rate and the B-17 had a crew of ten. The 91st lost 97 aircraft in combat and had 959 POWs. Simply multiplying the number of aircraft by the number of crew per aircraft and the bailout percentage will gives us the expected number of survivors on the ground, assuming a 100% success rate in the jump. Doing so gives us 985 expected survivors. Thus, from this method we get a baseline survivability rate of 97.4%.

A 97.4% survival rate for battlefield jumps may seem high, but it aligns closely with a review of American after-action reports. Because Americans bombed during the day, there is eyewitness testimony available to see how often airmen were able to pull the ripcords on their parachutes. During the most deadly missions of the 91st, after-action reports showed nearly 90% of observed airmen successfully deploying their canopies [11].

Using the same method for RAFBC is not as straightforward. Publicly available data is more difficult to find, so individual bomber groups cannot be used. This is problematic for one primary reason: the RAFBC used several different heavy bombers, including the famous Avro Lancaster, the Handley Page Halifax, the Short Shirley, the Avro Manchester, the Mosquito, and several others including American B-17s. The Halifax, Shirley, Lancaster and Manchester bombers had crews of seven. The Mosquito had a crew of two, while B-17's had a crew of ten. These different aircraft also had different bailout rates. In order not to overstate Cooper's chances at survival, conservative estimates for every variable will be used.

On the whole, RAFBC had a 21.3% bailout rate and lost 8,325 aircraft. Assuming six crew members per aircraft [12], the initial estimate for survivors is 10,640. In actuality there were 9,838 RAFBC POWs. The actual survival rate for bailing out using this method is 92.5%. This gives an approximate range of 79% to 93% for surviving a night time combat jump during World War II. This range overlaps with the numbers from the U.S. 91st Bomb Group, suggesting similar success rates for combat jumps regardless of if they were done in the daytime or at night.

The Parachute[43]

A possible confound in this analysis is the parachute itself. Cooper probably used a heavily modified NB6 parachute harness with a 28 foot canopy, owned by Earl Cossey [13]. The rip cord was moved from the left side to under the right armpit, somewhat hidden in a pocket. It would take two motions to deploy the canopy, first pushing the rip cord out from the chest, then sweeping the arm over the head. There is much conjecture over why Cossey modified the parachute to make it harder to deploy, but the likely reason was to avoid accidental deployment while in an aircraft packed with inexperienced skydivers [14]. It cannot be known how much these modifications would change Cooper's survival rate [15]. However, as is evidenced by the survival of thousands of RAF airmen, the difficulty of deploying a parachute while in free fall is negligible. Other than the specific location of the ripcord, the survival factors experienced by RAF night bomber crews is nearly identical to Cooper's. These WWII airmen jumped in the dark, after being exposed to freezing temperatures for many hours, with unfamiliar equipment and no jump training. The ability of these young men, who were under enemy fire, stumbling to fit through small emergency hatches in the dark to survive these circumstances, is strong endorsement of the human capacity to survive. While open to personal interpretation, the placement of the ripcord on the harness must pale in comparison to the difficulty of bailing out under the presented war scenarios.

The Drop Zone

An important factor in considering whether Cooper survived the jump is his actual drop zone. If Cooper landed in the deep

---

[43]This entire section dealing with the parachute can be ignored. FBI documents from the night of the hijacking confirm the two "back" parachutes belonged to Norman Hayden, a stunt-pilot with no interest or experience in skydiving. Hayden believes he gave two Pioneer parachutes to the FBI, eventually getting one back plus compensation for the parachute Cooper used. The FBI documents state one was a tan Pioneer, and the other a drab green NB6. In either case, both parachutes would not have been modified as Cossey suggested in the years before his murder.

woods of the Cascade Mountains or in Lake Merwin or another body of water, his survival chances go down precipitously. During the Normandy invasion, several groups of paratroopers were accidentally dropped offshore in the English Channel and drowned (Ryan, p 121). If Cooper lands on a pasture near a road within walking distance of a town, the reverse is true. While the exact landing spot can not be calculated with any certainty, a general drop zone can give insight into the Cooper mystery.

Much information about the flight path of 305 and the possible Cooper drop zone has either been lost or never existed. The FBI released a flight path, probably recorded by someone watching live radar data during the hijacking, and several independent Cooper investigators have analyzed the data [16]. One of the findings was a missing minute of a flight data, resulting in Cooper jumping between three and fifteen miles farther south than the original FBI search grid (Gray 2011, p 214 & 260). There is much debate about the significance of the "Missing Minute" so it will be used here only as an error estimate.

An air traffic controller stated firmly that 305 stayed in the Victor 23 corridor, which is about eight miles wide [17]. A small placard from flight 305 was found in the woods along the Victor 23 corridor. At 8:10pm the flight was near Ariel, WA. By 8:15pm, they were very near Portland, OR [18]. The plane was going approximately 190 mph and was traveling 3.1 miles per minute, ground speed. From crew testimony, we know the last communication was made with Cooper around 8:04 pm. After that, there was an oscillation, then a pressure bump around 8:13pm [19].

Using the FBI flight path, and adding in the forgotten minute, we get an approximate Cooper jump point near Battle Point [Figure 1]. Based on simple calculations using Google Earth, at 3.1 miles per minute, the Placard fell out of the plane around 8:03pm. Cooper and the cockpit communicated through the airplane's phone at around 8:04pm and the crew reported having difficulty hearing him due to the wind (Tosaw 1984, p35). Before this time, it appears Cooper was having difficulty lowering the stairs because he did not know you had to walk onto the stairs to counteract the force of the slipstream outside the plane (Gray, p 99-100).

While very scant, the evidence is in congruence with eyewitness testimony. Based on where the placard was found, Flight 305 was in Victor 23. Assuming the placard came out soon after Cooper learned "the trick" to the airstairs, the crew's timeline of events appears to be right. The 8:11 event represents a distinct feature of Cooper's walk down the stairs. As the stairs bumped up and down when Cooper worked his way to his jumping position, there were changes in pressure and flight characteristics, noted by the engineer. The final pressure bump, reproduced by the FBI in a later experiment, happens last, a few minutes after the oscillation. Generally assumed to happen sometime around 8:14pm (Rataczak, 2010).

The original FBI assessment, regardless of the missing minute, is accurate enough to eliminate the possibility of Cooper dropping in the Washougal watershed. It also makes it highly unlikely Cooper landed on the Tena Bar itself. Cooper likely left the aircraft between Orchards and Battleground, WA. This leaves the Tena Bar money find a perplexing event to describe through natural mechanisms alone. This also eliminates the Tena Bar find as definitive proof of Cooper's demise, unless some other evidence can bridge the gap between the crew's testimony and the find (see discussion).

Discussion

The probability that Cooper survived his jump is much higher than previously suggested. The experiences of thousands of RAF bomber crews in WWII show both the high danger of nighttime bailouts and the reliability of parachutes in those dangerous situations. Despite questions over the modifications of the parachute and how difficult pulling the ripcord would be for a novice in the dark, by underestimating Cooper's survival chances we are doing a disservice to the truth.

Understanding the high probability Cooper lived is also extremely important to interpreting other aspects of this case, especially the 1980 Tena Bar money find.

If the drop zone analysis is correct, Cooper landed farther south than the original 1971 estimate. He would have been within ten miles of Vancouver, in areas of flat farmland, not heavy woods or wilderness. The new drop zone increases the probability Cooper survived, assuming he pulled the ripcord, as it negates the need to survive and travel in the Northwest timber forests. A fit middle-aged man should be able to comfortably walk ten miles in day without taxing himself. Cooper would have thus been within walking distance of both bus and train stations. Since he got on Flight 305 at Portland, he likely was familiar enough with the area to transport himself away, just as he was able to transport himself to the area.

Though not the focus of this paper, the Tena Bar money find should be noted as it relates to Cooper's survival. Prima facie, it appears to be a contraindication of Cooper's survival. As Himmelsbach points out clearly, the money was the point of the whole adventure (Himmelsbach 1986, p 129). However, this assumes the money stayed with Cooper. In fact it is completely possible Cooper and the money separated during the jump. Once again, World War Two provides a clear illustration of the problem Cooper would have parachuting with a heavy bag of money.

Before the Normandy invasion, American paratroopers were given leg bags, also known as drop bags, just prior to their departure. They were not instructed how to properly use the bags, which were to be disconnected from the leg and lowered by the attached rope after their main canopy deployed. Many US paratroopers simply kicked the bags out of the aircraft as they jumped; when their main canopies deployed, the bags came loose and fell to the ground. Considering Cooper's improvised method for attaching the original money bag using paracord from one of the spare parachutes, it's not beyond reason to suggest the money was ripped from his harness when his canopy deployed [20].

The simplest explanation for the Tena Bar find, an explanation that requires the fewest non-natural elements to move the money from the drop zone to the sand bar, would be for the money to splash down in the Columbia River upstream from the original find. While it would take a major re-examination of the original timeline to get Cooper over the Columbia River at the time of the jump, it must be remembered the timeline is based mostly on eyewitness testimony. It is definitely possible, however unlikely, the crew was not accurate in their timing or misinterpreted the pressure events [21].

This is only conjecture, but if Cooper himself landed in water, even if he had pulled the ripcord on his parachute, his chances of surviving the jump are drastically lowered. Water landings, if a jumper is unprepared for them, are very lethal. Also, Cooper would have had to jump somewhere over Portland to land in the Columbia, and the crew generally believes Cooper was gone well before they crossed over the Columbia River. Regardless, since it is very possible that Cooper became separated from the money when his canopy deployed, the fate of the money is separate from the fate of Dan Cooper.

Since the money may have found its way to Tena Bar through any number of mechanical, natural or human processes, the crew testimony should take precedence over the money find when calculating a drop point. To use the money as the sole piece of evidence to dictate Cooper's drop zone is an example of the petitio principii fallacy. Until more facts are known, considering the intense investigation of the pressure bump event at the time, the initial assessment of a drop zone between the major water hazards of the jump are affirmed herein. Cooper's survival probability has not been adjusted to include a water landing.

Conclusions

There were numerous Cooper copycats, four of whom actually jumped out of their hijacked aircraft. All four hijackers survived their jumps. In particular, Robb Dolin Heady's jump was especially difficult; it was made while the aircraft was traveling, at his estimate, almost 300 miles per hour. It was his first night jump, and his first jet jump, and he only had a single reserve parachute [22]. In contrast, Cooper's aircraft was being held at a steady altitude, just above stall speed, and the pilots actually made adjustments at Cooper's request. Cooper's jump was done under close to ideal conditions. Of the five total 727 hijacking jumps, he would have been the most likely to survive.

The FBI assumption that Cooper died in the jump is based on poor data. Cooper jumped in conditions that thousands of RAF crewman survived during WWII. He jumped wearing a functional parachute, out of an aircraft the CIA was using to surreptitiously airdrop personnel and supplies. All four of his copycats survived their jumps. At a minimum, his survival chances were likely the same as the RAF bomber crews and they could be much higher. Based on everything noted so far, there is between an 80% and 90% chance Cooper pulled the ripcord on his parachute and landed safely somewhere along flight 305's path.

Bibliography

Gray, Geoffrey. (2011) Skyjack: The Hunt for D.B. Cooper. Crown. ISBN 0-307-45129-1

Himmelsbach, Ralph P.; Worcester, Thomas K. (1986). Norjak: The Investigation of D. B. Cooper. West Linn, Oregon: Norjak Project. ISBN 978-0-9617415-0-1.

Tosaw, Richard T. (1984) D.B. Cooper: Dead or Alive?. Tosaw Publishing. ISBN 0-9609016-1-2.

D. B. Cooper. (2014, November 24). In Wikipedia, The Free Encyclopedia. Retrieved 05:35, November 26, 2014, from http://en.wikipedia.org/w/index.php?title=D._B._Cooper&oldid=635293761

Rataczak, Bill. (2012) Hijacked! D.B. Cooper and Flight 305. DVD released by NWA History Center, inc.

Ryan, Cornelius. (1967) The Longest Day. Pocket Book Edition. ISBNs 1439126461, 9781439126462

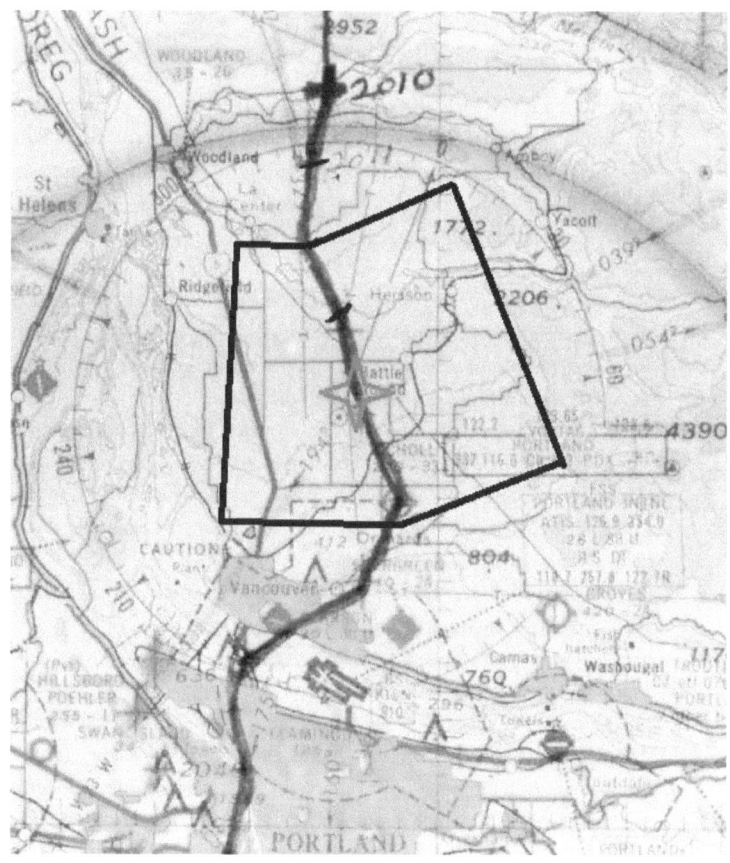

Figure 1. Estimated jumping point marked by red star; approximate landing zone outlined in black. Detail taken from FBI released flight path, from Citizen Sleuths website.

Notes

[1]Ralph Himmelsbach, the agent most associated with this case, has stated this numerous times in many popular publications and in his book Norjak. Case agent Larry Carr also implies this strongly in his many postings under the handle "Ckret" in the famous Drop Zone Cooper Forum (http://www.dropzone.com/cgi-bin/forum/gforum.cgi?post=3110098;sb= post_latest_reply;so=ASC;forum_view=forum_view_collapsed;guest=155049 508); A collection of Carr's posts on that forum are available as a pdf (http://collections. washingtonhistory.org/details.aspx?id=121550). Other case agents have not been so vocal, but the common narrative since at least the Tena Bar money find has been Cooper died.
[2]The Drop Zone Cooper Forum is a monster, totalling over 2000 pages with some 56,000 individual posts. It is difficult to navigate, and very hard to verify stories and expertise. However, it contains some of the best information available anywhere on the details of Cooper's jump, his equipment, and historical skydiving.
[3]These statistics were taken from the Wikipedia article on parachuting. And yes, I did check the original sources… And you can too:
http://www.uspa.org/AboutSkydiving/
SkydivingSafety/tabid/526/Default.aspx
[4]Seriously, literally every Cooper book references the jump conditions.
[5]Both Tosaw and Gray emphasize this fact in their books, whereas Himmelsbach mentions it only in passing. The case is strong, Cooper chose a military harness over a civilian model, and the FBI investigated 14,000 skydivers, and went undercover in Canadian skydiving competitions. If Cooper didn't get experience at a civilian facility, the assumption was he got it through the military. But we can't really be sure of anything; Tom Kaye points out the contradictions in understanding Cooper's jump experience rather elegantly: "He requested "front and back parachutes" = novice. He turned down instructions on how to use the parachute = experienced. He picked the non-steerable military parachute = novice. The military chute could better withstand the exit speed of the plane = experienced. He put the parachute on like he knew what he was doing = experienced. He took the reserve chute that was sewn closed and non-functional = novice."
(http://www.citizensleuths.com/db-cooper- what-you-need-to-know.html)
[6]RAF Bomber Command had casualties on par with WWI trench warfare. Source: http://www.elsham.pwp.blueyonder.co.uk/raf_bc/
[7]A discussion of the bailout differences between the various WWII bombers can be found in a 1979 book by Freeman Dyson called "Disturbing the Universe" which is a far reaching personal memoir encompassing Dyson's entire life. But… getting back to the point, this is a quote from his book on the hurdles facing RAF crews: "I shared an office at Command headquarters with a half-Irish boy of my own age called Mile O'Loughlin. One of the things that

Mike was angry about was escape hatches. Every bomber had a trap door in the floor through which the crew was supposed to jump when the captain gave the order to bail out. A far larger number died because they were inadequately prepared for the job of squeezing through a small hole with a bulky flying suit and parachute harness, in the dark, in a hurry, in an airplane rapidly going out of control. The mechanics of bailing out was another taboo subject which right-thinking crewmen were not encouraged to discuss. The actual fraction of survivors among the crews of shot-down planes was a secret kept from the squadrons even more strictly than the odds against their completing an operational tour."

[8]Complete story at http://www.veterans.gc.ca/eng/remembrance/those-who-served /diaries-letters-stories/second-world-war/watson, here's a snippet: "The flames were causing the seam aft of the starboard inner engine to melt and the pilot was informed of this, who then ordered everyone to collect their parachutes. The aircraft continued to lose height and the flames had enveloped most of the wing and half of the seam had melted, the pilot was informed of this and he ordered everyone to bail out. I then plugged into the intercom system and informed the pilot that he was bailing out and that the rear gunner was still in his turret and he would let him know we were getting out. The captain's last words to me were 'Yes, OK, but hurry, we're at 4,500 feet, if he's not hit he might make it. So long Ron, good luck.'"

[9]All data from my studies of RAF nighttime bailouts can be found here: (https://docs.google.com/document/d/1PZ7JHAGeWGupOZLihwJ9TG3kkrJW3qqg9wMmt-qBkPA/pub). This will also include any future data collections. Also, see note 7 too. And to belabor the point, here's another good article: http://www.express.co.uk/news/uk /399883/The-Lancaster-Bomber-that-magnificent-flying-machine

[10]Chosen for the availability of data online. Source: http://en.wikipedia.org/wiki/91st_Bombardment_Group

[11]In particular, missions 98, 229, 248, 275. After action reports (available at http://www.303rdbg.com/missions.html) showed 63 chutes for 70 observed bailouts.

[12]Full breakdown of RAFBC's aircraft are here: (https://docs.google .com/document/d /1PZ7JHAGeWGupOZLihwJ9TG3kkrJW3qqg9wMmt-qBkPA/pub).

[13]Cossey's ownership of the parachutes, and thus the nature of the modifications, is in dispute. http://themountainnewswa.net/2011/10/25/db-cooper-case-heats-up-again- with-controversy-over-parachutes/

[14]And you can find this discussion in the Drop Zone forum. Over like 2000 posts. Guru312 is the user handle of the person who described the possible reasons why Cossey modified his parachute.

[15]Skydivers display all the classic elements of being a clique, and I believe that is a large factor in why they underestimate Cooper's survival chances. On the skydiver forums, there is a lot of discussion about the difficulty of pulling a

ripcord while in free fall. They make it sound as though it is impossible to do unless you have paid $4000 for instructions on how to do so with a certified instructor. Whereas I believe this is mostly a product of Skydiver culture. Every RAF crew anecdote I read said they received absolutely no instruction on parachuting or pulling the ripcord in free fall. And yet most of those guys still pulled their ripcords. The debate factor is very high, but the central thesis of this paper is that the difficulties RAF crews faced were at least equal to, and probably much greater than the obstacles Cooper faced in his survival. Personally, I don't think Cossey's extensive modifications to the parachute would have changed Cooper's chances at all.

[16] Like, all of them.

[17] http://www.citizensleuths.com/flightpath.html

[18] Sluggo's Website on the hijacking includes a lot of great information about the flight path, http://n467us.com/index.htm.

[19] The separation of the pressure bump from the oscillation is conjecture on my part., mainly done to rectify the cockpit reports with the Tena Bar find. Rataczak does not report two distinct events, however the flight engineer might have reported a pressure change and an oscillation. The eyewitness testimony isn't clear.

[20] http://www.101airborneww2.com/equipment3.html

[21] My personal opinion is along these lines. Cooper jumped, lost the money when he pulled the ripcord, and was forced into hiding for the rest of his life. The money lands in the Columbia, where it quickly sinks to the bottom and gets slowly pushed along until a dredge chops up the bag and forces the two or three bundles of cash to the surface, where they remain buried for years. The dredge is not a popular mechanism based on Tom Kaye's findings, but evidence that the money was dredged comes from the fact money fragments were found all around Tena Bar, in depths of up to four feet: From around page 635 of the DZ forum: "'In that initial search they found "thousands of teeny shards of money the size of a man's fingernail, up to the size of a silver dollar." Dorwin said the pieces were well-preserved and layered in clean sand. "No matter how deep we dug we found money – homogeneously mixed to a great depth." Dorwin said that most agents were digging at a depth of 1.5-2 feet deep and that they dug at least four holes "at least four deep." He said they found shards in most holes and evenly placed all the way to the depth of four feet. " From an interview with Bruce Dorwin, FBI man on the site. Posted by snowman'

[22] http://themountainnewswa.net/2013/03/28/the-hunt-for-db-cooper-an-interview-with-a-so-called-cooper-copycat-skyjacker-robb-dolin-heady/

Special Thanks to Josh Taylor, Esq.

Copyright 2014 by Martin Andrade. Share freely with attribution.

FOIA Crew Debriefs

These documents were given to the DB Cooper Forum and were obtained through a FOIA request. The owner of the Cooper Forum Dave Brown says "the files were sent to me by a man known as Reichenbach, that's his username while on public forums. Credit needs to be given to him for supplying these documents." The files were later transcribed into a single document by an anonymous forum member. The names were originally redacted but were easily inferred by context. Emphases are mine. Some errors are inevitable in transcribing documents like these, the original scans are available at http://website.thedbcooperforum.com/Cooper-Vault/

Portland to SEA - Florence Schaffner 11/24/71

Florence Schaffner advised that she is a Stewardess employed by Northwest Orient Airlines and was serving in that capacity on NWA Flight No. 305 on November 24, 1971. Florence furnished the following information:

Florence said that she was standing at the rear entrance of the plane checking passengers in. She said that the man who she later identified as the hijacker was next to the last person to board the plane. She said that the man did not appear suspicious and did not attract her attention (when he boarded).

She said that after everyone had boarded the plane, she began serving refreshments while the plane was still parked in the terminal area. She said that the hijacker was the first person she served. She said he was sitting in Row #18, the last row of seats on the plane. She said the hijacker sat in the middle seat of three seats on the right-hand side of the plane, in the last row of seats on the plane.

Schaffner says that the man got her attention and reached up and handed her an envelope which she placed in her pocket. A short time later the man got her attention again and urged her to 'read the note'.

Schaffner said she opened the envelope while the plane was still taxiing toward the runway. She said the note inside the envelope was written in black felt-tip pen and read: "MISS - I have a bomb here and I would like you to sit by me."
MISS printed - rest in legible cursive.[44]
Schaffner said that she read the note twice and then looked up at the man. She said he was looking directly at her and she asked if he was kidding.

She said the man replied "No Miss, this is for real" in a serious but calm voice.

Schaffner passed the note to Mucklow who called front. Schaffner went and sat by the man who opened the brief case and showed her a bomb. He

---

[44] Writing a note like this in cursive is a minor point, but it's noteworthy as several Cooper suspects, including Barb Dayton, do not write in cursive.

showed her a wire INSIDE the case and he said 'touching this wire would detonate the bomb'! Man dictated his demands – Flo reached in her purse for pen and notepad. He said: **"No funny stuff or I'll do the job."** "After this we'll take a little trip." Schaffner got permission from the hijacker to take the notes to the pilot, Mucklow was on the interphone already talking to the cockpit, and Schaffner went to the cockpit with the notes. **Schaffner stayed in cockpit until plane landed.**

Mucklow sat with the passenger until they landed at Seattle, got his instructions, and then got up and went to front door and outside to get the money bag as instructed and brought down the aisle in front of passengers. Once the money was in Cooper allowed the passengers to leave. **When passengers gone Schaffner and Alice talked to Cooper while Mucklow went out to bring in the parachutes one or several at a time. Cooper remarked about how heavy the money was. He seemed amused and child-like (kind of detached from the seriousness of the situation).**

He offered her and Mucklow the change from his pocket- the $20 bill change for the drink, but Schaffner told him: "We don't accept tips". Schaffner said the man spoke of going to Mexico City, Phoenix, or San Francisco. She said that he did not appear to know exactly where he was destined for. She asked if they (stews) were going to go with him but he did not reply. She finally asked if the stews could leave the plane and the man replied "Sure go ahead" in a calm uninterested manner.

She said that by this time the man had begun putting on one of the back parachutes, and at some time during their conversation he put on a pair of sunglasses.

Schaffner described the hijacker as follows:
Race White. Sex Male. Age mid 40's. Height 6'0". Weight 170-175 lbs. Build: Average. Eyes Brown. Hair: Black, medium length, straight, parted on the left side.
Complexion: Olive type.
Clothing: Black business suit, white shirt, thin

black tie, black overcoat, black shoes. Was carrying a black business man's type briefcase described as ordinary. Had a pair of dark framed sunglasses with dark brown lenses.

She said the man appeared to be of Latin descent with no distinguishing characteristics such a scars, marks, or tatoos. She said the man had no moustache or beard and spoke in a normal calm voice. She saw no rings or jewelry.

Schaffner furnished 13 pages of notes which she took during the course of the flight.

11/24/71 Hancock Interview:

Alice Hancock a stewardess aboard Northwest Airlines Flight #305 provided the following information:

On November 24, 1971, Hancock stated that the individual who hijacked Northwest Airlines Flight #305, a Boeing 727, boarded the aircraft at Portland OR, and at the time he boarded he was carrying a briefcase which measured about 12 by 18 inches, and was dark brown or black in color. She stated that the hijacker handed another stewardess (Florence Schaffner) a ransom note demanding $200,000 dollars in cash. Hancock believes that the note was handed to Schaffner very shortly before takeoff from Portland. Hancock advised that the hijacker's demands were communicated to the Captain of the aircraft via the aircraft's intercom by another stewardess named Mucklow.

Hancock stated that the note the hijacker handed to Schaffner stated the hijacker had a bomb, in a briefcase he was carrying, and that he wanted $200,000 dollars and absolutely no trickery or interference or he would explode the bomb he said he was carrying. Hancock also advised the hijacker requested four parachutes. After the hijacker stated these demands, the stewardess named Schaffner went to the cockpit of the aircraft (with the note the hijacker had written and another list of his demands she had written as the hijacker dictated his demands to her), to advise the Captain of the plane of the situation. (In the meantime another stewardess named Mucklow took a seat beside the hijacker). Stewardess Schaffner remained in the cockpit remained in the cockpit until just before landing in Seattle. Meanwhile the hijacker remained in his seat and had another stewardess named Mucklow sit by him.

Hancock stated the hijacker assigned the stewardess named Mucklow to get off the plane in Seattle to get the money he demanded, and then after that she was to go off the airplane again and get four parachutes that he demanded. In addition to the parachutes and the money the

hijacker also requested four crew meals.[45] Hancock says that 'Flo' had told her that he hijacker wanted to go to Mexico and was very concerned throughout the flight about Sky Marshals being on board the aircraft.

Hancock stated that the subject made his demands known in this order:
1. He wanted the money brought on board first.
2. We wanted (passengers) off the aircraft after the money was on board.
3. We wanted parachutes and four crew meals.
4. He wanted the plane completely refueled.
5. We wanted maps.

She could not remember what kind of maps the subject requested.[46]

During the flight, Hancock advises the hijacker wanted continual re-assurance that nothing was going to go wrong. She stated that the hijacker was good natured during the flight.

After the plane landed (at Seattle) and the passengers were off-loaded, Mucklow was on the telephone updating the hijacker's demands to the Captain of the aircraft.

The hijacker then informed Mucklow to tell the other stewardesses and crew to remain on board. At this point Hancock states that the pilots of the aircraft wanted the stewardesses off the plane. (They tried to arrange this with the hijacker through Mucklow). Once the stewardesses were off the aircraft, Hancock states that the pilots had planned to get off the aircraft by jumping out through (a door in) the cockpit. (The hijacker however would not let Mucklow come forward).[47]

---

[45] Cooper consistently showed a high degree of empathy to the crew. This is odd, and something FBI SA Larry Carr picked up on; bank robbers don't normally offer tips to their victims.

[46] These maps are something of a mystery. It's possible the FBI has more information about them. It is known the cockpit crew were given aeronautical maps for the flight.

[47] First Officer Bill Rataczack is adamant in his interviews that they did have opportunity to leave the aircraft, but that Schaffner and Hancock missed the opportunity.

None of this happened because the hijacker could see them and they feared that he would set off the bomb that he had in his briefcase.

The Schaffner went to the back of the plane and asked the hijacker directly if the stewardesses could go and he said: Whatever you girls would like". Then Hancock and Schaffner left the plane with Mucklow still in the back with the hijacker. Hancock describes the subject as a male Caucasian, olive complexion, age 38-45, 6'1", 170-175 lbs, slim build, black hair, wavy (marcelled) and short on the back (Continental look?), He wore no hat and wore sunglasses with plastic frames **which looked like prescription glasses.** He wore a black trench coat, white shirt and tie, and dark slacks. He wore no gloves and was soft-spoken and had no accent. He had no visible scars or marks. Hancock states that he had his hand inside the brief case at all times when he and Mucklow we seated together in row 18.

(During her final minutes on board and after the parachutes had been brought aboard), Hancock noticed that one of the parachutes had been unpacked and she asked the hijacker if he had taken the parachute apart and he replied "yes". Hancock says the hijacker began unpacking one chute and cutting cords almost as soon as the chutes were brought on board.

Interview 11-30 Mucklow:

Tina Mucklow was interviewed at the Reno Airport, Reno Nevada, in the late evening of November 24, 1971, and during the early morning hours of November 25th, 1971, She identified herself as a hostess on the Northwest Airlines Flight #305, that was hijacked.

Shortly after takeoff from Portland en route to Seattle, in the afternoon hours of November 24, 1971, a male passenger on the flight who was seated in 18-E, gave a note to Hostess Florence Schaffner. Schaffner showed the note to Hostess Mucklow who was also in the rear passenger compartment. The note indicated that the male passenger was hijacking the plane and wanted the hostess (Schaffner) to sit beside him. The note further indicated that he had a bomb and wanted $200,000.

Mucklow stated that she went back to the male passenger seated in 18-E with the note, and which time (the hijacker) indicated that he was hijacking the plane and 'was not kidding'. He added that he wanted "no funny stuff". He had a black attaché-type case in his lap which was partially open and he had his hand inside (the case). At this time Mucklow sat down beside the individual in seat 18-D and after lighting a cigarette for the passenger, she told him that they would cooperate. Her best recollection is that it was while he told her he wanted no "funny stuff" that he partially opened the briefcase more and he permitted her to see the contents (of the case).[48]

She recalls the contents of the case as approximately eight cylindrical objects about six to eight inches long with four of the items being placed on top of the others and banded together with (black) tape. She also recalls some covered and uncovered wiring running from the cylindrical objects to a dry cell type battery which had terminals on one end. She could not recall if the

---

[48]Both Mucklow and Florence Schaffner were allowed to see the bomb.

wires were connected to the terminals. The battery was described as approximately eight inches long and about two and one-half in diameter. She states that she had the impression seeing the contents that (it could be) dynamite; however, she is unfamiliar with the (exact) appearance of dynamite and could only describe it as stated above, adding that it (the sticks) were a "reddish rusty color".

Mucklow says (she got up) and advised the pilot's compartment via the intercom, that the plane was being hijacked. She used the interphone while remaining in her seat because she could reach it from her seated position. She used a pre-arranged signal of bells that signaled the pilot's compartment. Mucklow then used a plain envelope to write out the demands of the hijacker, listing that he wanted four parachutes including two back packs and two chest packs, $200,000 in cash in small bills, and that he wanted everything by "by five o'clock". Mucklow says that Florence Schaffner delivered this note to the pilot's compartment, since the hijacker insisted that she stay physically present beside him at all times. She says that she sat with the hijacker from then through almost the whole time from then on (until she as released by the hijacker to go forward to the cockpit).

Mucklow recalled that during the flight from Portland to Seattle, all passengers were moved at least three rows forward from the back row where the hijacker was seated. At one time the subject stated that the bomb he had was electrically fused and he certainly hoped the crew would not generate any electrical currents which would trigger it!

In response to her query as to why he had chosen a Northwest airplane to hijack, he said **'he had "a grudge but not against Northwest Airlines"** adding **'that the Northwest plane just happened to be in the right place at the right time'**.

In response to her query during their conversation as to where he came from, Mucklow says the hijacker was adamant in his refusal to answer and seemed somewhat provoked by the question.

Frequently during her conversation with the hijacker he kept reminding her that the crew should "nothing funny" and each time she reassured him that he would receive the full cooperation of the crew.

He instructed Mucklow that upon landing she was to be his (only) intermediary in not only delivering messages to the crew but also in transferring items that he had requested from the ground, to him in the aircraft. He was insistent that every condition be met and that everything be available on the ground prior to the landing of the aircraft.

Mucklow says the hijacker went to the lavatory when the plane landed stating he would return in a few minutes, at which time the stairway to the forward door should be ready. When he went to the lavatory he closed the (briefcase) and carried it with him. He came out of the lavatory in a matter of three or four minutes and took the same seat he had occupied before.[49]

(When she received the bag containing the money on the ground) She took the bag containing the money back to seat 18-E where the hijacker was seated.

He opened the bag and inspected the contents which Mucklow said she observed was money packed in small packages with bank-type bands around each package. Having inspected the money in a cursory fashion the hijacker stated that "it looks ok" and then indicated to Mucklow that the crew could now let the passengers deplane. She stated that she called the cockpit on the intercom with this message and an announcement was made from the cockpit that passengers could disembark.

Mucklow recalls that at this time while the passengers were unloading, in an attempt at being humorous, she suggested to the hijacker 'that there was obviously a lot of money in the bag and could she have some'! The hijacker agreed with her suggestion and reached in and took out one package

---

[49]Some claim Cooper spent a lot of time in the Lav to avoid the possibility of sniper fire, but this makes it very clear he was just going to the bathroom.

of the money, denominations not recalled by Mucklow, **and he handed the (single) bundle of money to her!** Mucklow states that she laughed and gave the money back to the hijacker stating 'she was not permitted to accept gratuities', or words to that effect.[50] In a similar vein Mucklow recalls that at one time during the flight the hijacker had pulled some single bills from his pocket (change from a $20 he was given earlier for a drink he had purchased) and attempted to (give the bills back) to tip the girls on the crew. (He was told then they could not accept tips). So again, they declined in compliance with company policy.

After the passengers deplaned, Mucklow stated that in accordance with the instructions from the hijacker, she went to get the parachutes he had requested. She brought back one large parachute (back pack) first, stating that she could only carry one parachute of this kind at a time. It was after she brought this first parachute into the aircraft that he told her to lower all the window shades in his section of the aircraft. After pulling down these shades Mucklow then left the aircraft and brought back two smaller parachute packs (chest packs) and gave these to the hijacker. She then made a last trip from the aircraft to obtain (the last of) the large parachutes (a back pack). All of the parachutes were given to the hijacker and Mucklow observed him looking them over as she left them with him. She says that at this time all hostesses and male crew members were still aboard the aircraft. At this point Mucklow recalls bringing up with the hijacker what the instructions were regarding the future destination of the flight; up to this point he had refused to tell her where he would order the flight to go. At this time, he told her not to worry, the flight was not going to Havana but it would go to a "pleasant place".

Mucklow says that she got one of her pay sheets and had a pencil and took down the following instructions from the hijacker:

---

[50] Cooper offered a tip at least twice to the stewardesses.

Going to Mexico City - - or any place in Mexico - - nonstop - - gear down - - flaps down - - don't go over 10,000 feet altitude - - all cabin lights out - - do not again land in the United States for fuel or any other reason - - no one is to come behind the first class section."

Mucklow forwarded this information to the cockpit (via the intercom) and the hijacker also indicated he wanted takeoff made with the rear door open and the stairs extended at takeoff. He had also indicated that in addition to the passengers, all of the hostesses would be allowed to exit the aircraft prior to taking off.

The hijacker further indicated to Mucklow that as soon as this lowering of the door and stairs was accomplished in flight, she would be permitted to go to the pilot's compartment. It was during the period of furnishing these conditions the hijacker became extremely annoyed over the time it was taking to refuel the plane, as he had ordered.

The hijacker displayed an extensive knowledge of the aircraft and seemed specifically well informed in refueling procedures to the point that the crew had difficulty in convincing him that only 90% of the required fuel was on board at the time he was protesting the fact that refueling had not been completed. It was also during this time that he complained to Mucklow that he had requested the money be delivered in a knapsack but instead it was delivered in a cloth type bank bag, which displeased him. **It was at this time that Mucklow recalls he stated he would be forced to use one of the parachutes to rewrap the money since he had not been furnished the knapsack.**[51] At this same time Mucklow says she suddenly **observed him having a small green paper bag, contents unknown.**[52] She

---

[51] It can't be known exactly what Cooper meant by this, since he was seen wrapping the canvas bank bag in paracord, but he may have split the money between the bank bag and the other reserve container at this point.

[52] I stated earlier that I believed this green bag was actually canvas and that Cooper brought it specifically to attach to his harness to help secure all of his stuff to him for the jump. I waver on this, though. The bag may just be a bakery bag with Cooper's lunch. Clara says she saw a green canvas bag with about half the money in it, which menas she likely saw the reserve container.

states that she recalled no other packages or luggage belonging to the hijacker except for the briefcase and this small green paper bag. She says it was also about this time she again offered the hijacker something to eat or drink, which he refused. She recalls that (other than the original bourbon he ordered when he first boarded and was served) **he accepted no refreshments or food of any kind while he was on the aircraft.**

Mucklow also recalled it was at this time that the hijacker requested that all notes, including the one he had furnished to Schaffner and those written by Schaffner be returned to him. Likewise, she said he was a chain smoker and at one time she had lit a cigarette for him with the last match in a paper match folder he provided. When she attempted to discard the empty match folder the hijacker decisively took it from her and placed in one of his pockets stating he did not want her to throw it away. She recalled that he smoked Raleigh filter tips.

Mucklow states that the hijacker was concerned about the time it was taking to collect items requested in his demands. He commented that (he thought) **'the parachutes were coming from McChord Air Force Base', even though the crew had said nothing about this. The hijacker remarked that it was 'only about 20 minutes from McChord to the Seattle-Tacoma Airport', his words.** She said that while they were in the holding pattern over Seattle, the hijacker at one point looked out the window and observed **"We're over Tacoma now"**. **(Was this true?) Mucklow wonders if the hijacker was familiar with the area?**

Mucklow says that after refueling and takeoff was imminent, the flight crew called on the intercom and reported that due to the flying conditions the hijacker had set, the fuel load would not permit them to fly nonstop to Mexico City, or anywhere as far away as Mexico for that matter. The crew suggested the fuel range would allow San Francisco. **The hijacker countered with Ploenix, Arizona** but the flight crew said 'no' due to the distance. The hijacker stated the aircraft could make Yuma, Arizona or Reno, Nevada **and he stated he preferred landing at Reno, Nevada. The crew called back and approved Reno and said they would proceed to Reno, Nevada.**

Mucklow states that at takeoff from Seattle the hijacker was in seat 18-D or 18-E, occupying both seats at various times, and she was seated across the aisle in 18-C. Mucklow states that at takeoff the hijacker was using several seats and **was occupied with opening one of the parachutes and attempting to pack the money in the parachute container and attach it to his body using the parachute (container's) straps.** Mucklow recalls that the parachute was a bright pink-orange color. Mucklow's description is somewhat vague but she says **he removed a small jack-knife from his pocket and he cut some portion of the outside container or the parachute in order to secure the money in 'this' rather than in the white cloth type bank bag which had been furnished him.** She says that she did not see him tamper with the two large parachute containers other than to generally inspect them when she brought them aboard.

After the plane was airborne, there was conversation between Mucklow and the hijacker regarding her opening the rear door and extending the stairway. She told him she was fearful of being sucked out of the airplane and, wanted to tie an emergency safety rope around her waist and attach it to the seat… **The subject told her it would not be necessary for her to use a safety rope but he would cut one of the parachute lines to insure her safety when she opened the door.**[53] At this same time he was still working with the parachute (container and lines) to in some way secure the money to his body.

Shortly thereafter he asked her to demonstrate the procedure for opening the rear door and extending the stairway. She did this and was under the impression that he understood her instructions. She says it occurred to her at this time that this was the only function of the aircraft which she had discussed with the hijacker

---

[53]Rataczak claims in this was his idea in the History Channel interview.

which he did not seem to be fully aware of.⁵⁴ She stated as a matter of fact, **he had even shown a knowledge of where the oxygen bottles were, at an earlier time.** While she could not recall specifically, **she stated there were several other comments he made which gave her the impression that he had an extensive technical knowledge of this particular type of aircraft and flying in general.** She also commented that he appeared to be **completely familiar the parachutes which had been furnished to him.**

It is estimated by Mucklow that in less than five minutes after takeoff, the hijacker suddenly told her to go forward, to close the curtain behind her, and not to return to the rear compartment again. She quickly complied with this request going to the first class cabin, closing the curtain behind her, then proceeding to the cockpit and closing and locking the cockpit door behind her. She did not thereafter leave the pilot's compartment and had no further contact with the hijacker face to face to via intercom.

Mucklow furnished the following description, it being noted that she is approximately 5'8" in height and she observed the hijacker in a seated position except for the brief period when he was up and went to the lavatory. She says at no time did he remove the dark glasses he was wearing and was never able to observe his eyes or eyebrows.

Race: white, Sex, Male, Age Mid 40's, Height: 5'10" to 6', Weight: 180-190 lbs., Build: medium well built, Hair: dark brown had sideburns partially past his ears, hair parted and combed back, Complexion: Medium, smooth, Characteristics: Wore dark rimmed wrap-around glasses with black frames, concealed eyes entire time, had no accent possibly from West or Midwest, had a low voice;

Clothing: dark top coat, brown suit, brown shoes, black tie with tie tack found on plane was possibly his.

---

⁵⁴This almost certainly eliminates Kenny Christiansen as a suspect. Christiansen would have known how to deploy these stairs.

11-24 Harold Anderson:

Harold E Anderson, was interviewed at the Reno Airport, Reno Nevada, late on the evening of November 24, 1971. He identified himself as the Third Officer & Flight Engineer on Northwest Airlines Flight #305.

Anderson advised that according to some notes he made, it was at 2759 Zulu time or 3:59 pm Pacific Standard Time, that he received an emergency signal from hotess Mucklow on the interphone with a series of bells signalling they had trouble onboard. This is a pre-arranged signal for such emergencies and he made a notation in his book of the time of notification.

Almost immediately (in tandem with Mucklow's signal) he received a note from Hostess Schaffner, advising she thought they were being hijacked and she added she was "not kidding"! Soon after Hostess Mucklow brought in a note on standard 6x9 tablet paper written with a felt tip pen as well as an envelope that had notations on it noting the figure "$200,000, two back pack parachutes, two chest packs" and under it "by 5:00pm".

Hostess Mucklow then went back to the rear compartment and sat with the hijacker at which time he (the hijacker) (communicated again through Mucklow on the interphone) that 'all of the above items be physically present and waiting at the Seattle Airport upon our arrival and prior to landing'.

Mucklow received the impression that this hijacking was carefully planned and thought out in advance in that the hijacker was even specifying that the money was to be furnished in a knapsack and even had already insisted that a discarded matchbook cover (he had provided for one of the stews to light a cigarette for him) be returned to him. The hijacker was also insisting on the return of his original note and envelope given to Schaffner, and was being especially careful to see that nothing was left behind.

Anderson stated that as soon as they verified the intentions of the hijacker they immediately contacted the company via their radio connections, concerning the situation, but they did not alert the passengers or press the emergency transponder code button, signaling a hijacking to the control towers, due to the hijacker's insistence of "no funny stuff".

They subsequently radioed the Seattle Approach Control Tower and requested holding instructions in order that they could remain airborne for the approximate 1½ hours which they estimated would be required in order to fulfil all of the demands the hijacker had stipulated.

Anderson notes that all of the demands were forwarded to to the cockpit by the hostesses Mucklow and Schaffner and at no time did he (Anderson) have an occasion to personally observe or have any contact with the hijacker.

Since Seattle was the original destination of the flight, an announcement was made from to the passengers from the cockpit that they were going to enter a holding pattern to burn off excess fuel, which helped put the passengers at ease. In addition, the hostesses were instructed not to serve any additional drinks to any of the passengers.

It was further established that Hostess Mucklow was to act as a intermediary between the hijacker and the individuals meeting the plane, to supply his demands. The Chief Pilot for Northwest Airlines and one other individual were to be in the first vehicle with the money, the second vehicle was to carry the stairs so the hostess could exit from the front of the plane, with only one driver designated for that vehicle, **and a third vehicle being a fuel truck containing a driver only which was to remain in a 10 or 11 o'clock position from the plane in order that all would be in full view of the hijacker at all times.**

After the plane had landed and the delivery of the money and parachutes, the hijacker forwarded through hostess Mucklow the following instructions: (1) ... going to Mexico City non-stop or if they could not reach Mexico City then anywhere in Mexico, (2) … fly with landing gear and flaps down, (3) not fly above 10,000 feet, (4) … lights out in the cabin area, (5) they were not to land in the USA for fuel or any other reason, (6) nobody is allowed aft of the first class curtain, (7) … after taking off hostess Mucklow will be allowed to go to the cockpit, (8) the rear door is to be open and the stairs extended for taking off.

We informed the hijacker that under the conditions that he had stipulated, it would be impossible to reach Mexico City and he countered with the possible destination of Phoenix. He then mentioned a number of destinations which were considered and rejected which included Yuma, Sacramento, and finally Reno was reached as the final destination we would go to…

Anderson recalls that after initially receiving descriptive data from the hostess Schaffner, they radioed the company for any likely suspects or modus operandi and the company furnished the name of a _____ Cooper who had previously been arrested for being intoxicated et cetera…

Anderson stated that the departure from Seattle was made at 7:36pm[55] and at about 8:05 pm he called the hijacker on the interphone and inquired if he could hear ok and whether there was anything they could do for him? The hijacker responded in the negative and the crew decided against any more tests or contacts until they arrived at Reno, Nevada, that the hijacker was on board for the duration of the flight. Upon approaching Reno Airport, they tried to contact the hijacker with no response and they notified their company of the same.

Anderson stated that approximately 5 to 10 minutes after the last contact with subject at 8:05 pm, they heard and felt an oscillation of the aircraft and commented that the hijacker could have departed causing the unusual vibration since there had been no change in flight parameters or

---

[55]Estimates for the actual takeoff of 305 from Seattle range from 7:34pm to 7:40pm. Anderson's estimate matches other reliable documentation and should be used as the true takeoff time.

any other external force which would account for this sudden vibration. They telephoned the company representative (_____ in _____) shortly thereafter and stated that the 'oscillation' which could have been the hijacker's departure, would have occurred between 8:05 pm and their call to the company 5 or ten minutes later, **the exact time being recorded in the company log.**[56] **Anderson stated that they had not reached Portland proper but were definitely in the suburbs or immediate vicinity thereof.**

Anderson added that no member of the crew went back to check on the presence of the hijacker immediately following the 'oscillations' the crew encountered. When the subject let hostess Mucklow go to the cockpit she locked the door behind her. Anderson added, **it had not occurred to them at the time to pinpoint their exact location at the time of the oscillation** …

---

[56] This time is recorded as between 8:10pm and 8:11pm

Interview of Mucklow 12/1-2 at her home in PA:

Tina Mucklow, residing at the home of her family, provided the following information: On November 24th 1971, while employed as a stewardess for Northwest Airlines, Ms. Mucklow was on Flight No. 305 which originated in Washington DC, and arrived at Minneapolis Minn about 10:00 a.m., and Ms Mucklow boarded shortly thereafter. She says the crew for her flight was Pilot Wm Scott, Co-pilot Wm 'Bill' Rataczak, Third officer and Engineer Harold 'Andy' Anderson, Senior Stewardess Alice Hancock, B Stewardess Florence Schaffner, and finally C Stewardess (herself) Tina Mucklow, the junior member of the crew.

Mucklow advised that her flight departed Minneapolis at 10:35 am CST with a light load of less than half its compliment of passengers, flew to Great Falls, Montana, then to Missoula, Montana, and then to Spokane, Washington, and then Portland, Oregon. She said that the aircraft departed Portland at 2:53 pm Pacific Standard Time, and arrived two hours and fifty three minutes later at Seattle, Washington, which is normally a 36 minute flight.

Just before the Second Officer (Rataczak) gave the word for takeoff from Portland, Hostess Schaffner took a beverage form to the aft jump seat. There was a man in seat 18-E middle after passenger seat, and as Mucklow faced the barrier strip, she observed Hostess Schaffner dropping a note, stand up and she unfastened the barrier strip and sat down next to the man in seat 18-E. **Mucklow says that Hostess Schaffner appeared 'emotional' in that she was trying to speak to her (Mucklow), was moving her lips, but other than a gasp, no other words no other words came out.**

Mucklow picked up the note lying at her feet and read it. To the best she can remember, it said: "Miss. I am hijacking this plane. I have a bomb. Sit next to me."

The aircraft listed off the runway at 2:58pm and Mucklow used the interphone to advise the pilot the plane was being hijacked. She said: We're being hijacked, he's got a bomb, and this is no joke." Mucklow replaced the phone and leaned down in the aisle near Schaffner and saw her writing something on an envelope. After Schaffner finished writing she said to the man next to her that she would take the note to the cockpit. Mucklow says she asked Schaffner if she wanted her to take the note forward and Schaffner said "no". Mucklow asked "Do you want me to stay here?" and the man replied, "yes". Schaffner then took the note forward to the cockpit.

Mucklow sat next to the man and shortly thereafter he opened a black cheap appearing imitation leather attache case and showed her a device, with eight red cylinders and a wire running from the cylinders toward a large 6x8x2" battery. The wire had a red plastic coating on it except for the last inch which was bare and the man was holding between his fingers. **He told (me) it was an electronic device and suggested the aircraft radio be used as little as possible. He then said 'he didn't think radio transmissions would bother it, but he wanted the crew warned'.**

(After these statements from the hijacker) Mucklow called the pilot over the interphone and advised him of the device (and the hijacker's statements) and from that point on she acted as the communications intermediary, between the hijacker and the pilot using the interphone. (When Mucklow became intermediary there was some confusion about what had transpired before and the hijacker's demands).

During one message to the pilot the hijacker specified that all of the previously requested items be at the airport when he landed. Mucklow later learned that the note which Schaffner had carried to the pilot contained a list of (specific) demands. The hijacker later told (repeated to) Mucklow that he wanted $200,000 in circulated US currency, two back and two front parachutes, and fuel trucks to meet the plane when it landed. One of the specific demands that he made was that the fuel was to come first and start fueling the plane immediately. Everyone in the plane was to remain in their seats and he indicated that Mucklow was to be the liaison and the one to go out and get the money and the parachutes. After fueling was completed and the money was on board, the hijacker indicated that the passengers would be released, and the last item to be brought aboard would be the chutes, and that only the crew members were to be aboard and they must stay out of the aisle and remain in their seats.

During the flight from Portland to Seattle Mucklow had light conversation with the hijacker. She asked him where he was from but he became upset and said he didn't want to answer that. She steered the conversation into remarking 'that if they were going to Cuba airline personnel were advised to warn passengers against buying Cuban rum or cigars because US Customs would confiscate them when they returned to the United States.

(Mucklow says) the hijacker laughed and said 'they weren't going to Cuba, but she would like where they were going'.

He asked her where she was from and she told him she was from Pennsylvania but was living in Minneapolis. **He replied that 'Minneapolis, Minnesota is very nice country'.**

She asked him why he picked Northwest Airlines to hijack and he laughed and said "**It's not because I have a grudge against your airlines (plural), it's just because I have a grudge". He paused and said 'that the flight suited his time, place, and plans.'**

Other conversation centered around personal habits such as smoking and he asked her if she did and she said she used to but quit, and he offered her a cigarette which she took and smoked. She asked him if he wanted any food or drink and he refused everything.

During the flight from Portland to Seattle, a male passenger started aft down the aisle and Mucklow met him at about Row 14. She asked him what he wanted and he replied 'he was looking for a sports magazine'. Mucklow took him to the aft section of the plane immediately behind the hijacker where they looked and finally he accepted a New Yorker Magazine, and returned to his seat. After the man was seated Mucklow returned to seat 18-D, next to the hijacker, and he said "If that is a Sky Marshall I don't want any more of that", and Mucklow reassured the hijacker it wasn't (a sky marshal) and further 'that there are no sky marshals on this flight'.

A short time later the pilot called and asked Mucklow to ask the hijacker if he wanted the passengers informed of the situation, and the hijacker said "No". The pilot replied that he would come up with an excuse to explain the extension of the flight beyond its normal 36 minutes. It was at this point that the hijacker instructed Mucklow to tell the pilot he wanted his note and envelope back. He also wanted the empty matchbook cover from which he had been lighting his cigarettes; Mucklow had thrown that into the trash pouch on the seat in front of 18-D where you would normally throw personal trash. Mucklow indicated he had another similar book of matches and the cover was **blue and said "Sky Chef"**. He retained that book of matches in his pocket. While in the holding pattern over Seattle the hijacker noted: 'It is 5:15 and we are still waiting. I wanted everything by 5:00 o'clock!'

Mucklow called the pilot on the phone and got an update and informed the hijacker 'we are waiting for the front pack chutes to arrive at the airport from McChord'. The hijacker replied: **"McChord is only 20 minutes from Tacoma; it doesn't take that long."** Mcklow called the pilot again and the crew said the chutes were 'en route' and the cockpit requested permission from the hijacker to start the descent without the chutes being present at the airport. The hijacker said "yes provided the chutes are there by the time the fueling is completed". A few minutes later the pilot called back and advised 'the chutes have arrived and we are going to land'.

The flight landed at Seattle International Airport at 5:45pm Pacific time. Prior to the landing the pilot wanted permission from the hijacker to park the aircraft away from the terminal and the hijacker said "ok". The pilot said he would park in a semi-lighted runway not being used and this pleased the hijacker. While the aircraft was being taxied to that area Mucklow asked the hijacker's permission to move five passengers away from the area of seat row 18 and the hijacker approved of that.

Stewardess Mucklow stood at Row 15 in the middle of the isle to make certain no one came aft. When the aircraft stopped the pilot got permission from the hijacker to let the fuel trucks approach the plane. The stairs truck came to the front door and Mucklow left via the front door and went to the car carrying the money, chutes, food, maps, and a radio for cockpit communications. At this time the hijacker got up and went to the aft lavatory. When Mucklow returned the hijacker was back in his seat. Mucklow dragged a white canvas money bag down the aisle (right in front of the passengers) to where the hijacker was sitting and placed it on seat 18-D next to the hijacker. The hijacker looked through the bag and said that it was 'now alright for the passengers to get off the plane'. Mucklow notified the pilot and the pilot made an announcement 'the passengers could now leave the aircraft'.

After the passengers left Mucklow asked the hijacker if he wanted her to get the other items waiting outside and he said "yes", but he wanted the other crew members to remain seated. Mucklow then left and brought in one large parachute (back pack). The hijacker told her to lower the window shades, which she did. Mucklow then left again and brought in two small chutes (front packs). Her next trip she got the last 'big chute' and placed it with the others in Row 18. **At this time Mucklow handed him a sheet of instructions on 'how to jump and use a parachute' and he said 'he didn't need that'.** Prior to all of this Mucklow asked the hijacker if he wouldn't rather have one of the cockpit crew (men) get the chutes, but the **hijacker told her 'they aren't that heavy and she** wouldn't have any trouble'.

When Mucklow returned to the plane with the last back pack chute, **she saw that the hijacker had one of the small chutes open and was cutting nylon cords out with his pocket knife. He took the nylon cord and wrapped it around the neck of the money bag numerous times and then he wrapped it a few times from top to bottom, and with the same piece (of cord) he made a loop like a handle at the top. This nylon cord was pinkish in color. He appeared irritated that they hadn't given him a knapsack for the money as requested, and after trying to put the money in an unfolded parachute, he decided to leave it in the canvas bag (and fabricate a holding line for that, instead).**[57]

She told him that they had crew meals and maps, and requested permission to go get them. He replied "yes" and Mucklow went to get the items and returned taking a seat next to him.

He said, "We're going to Mexico City, gear down, flaps down, **you can trim the plane to 15**[58], you can stop anywhere in Mexico to refuel, but not here in the United States. The aft door must be open and the stairs down. The altitude, under 10,000 feet, they know they can't go over that. Cabin lights out and everyone is to be forward of the first class curtain."

Mucklow relayed these instruction to the pilot. **Hancock came back to where the hijacker was seated and asked if she could get could get her purse. The hijacker said she could come on back, he wouldn't bite her. Then she asked if the stewardesses could get off an he said "yes"**

About one hour had passed since landing and Mucklow was taking information for the hijacker from the pilot and she told the other stewardesses to go ahead and she would be with them in a

---

[57]This is Mucklow's second interview, and her description here is different from her earlier interview. In the earlier interview, she does not describe this act of wrapping the bank bag in paracord.

[58]This is the first time it is mentioned that the hijacker requested flaps being set to a distinct setting. In his DVD talk, Rataczak says he asked the hijacker over the phone what the flap settings should be (possibly he did this through Tina) and the hijacker replied "15 degrees."

second, and they went forward to the cockpit. She told the hijacker that the plane 'could not' take off with the ladder down and he said in a low voice: **"Yes they can, but the cockpit can put it down after they get airborne.**[59]**"** She told him that the stairs had to be let down from the rear and at this point he appeared disturbed because of the duration of time the refueling was taking, and he told her to stay (with him).

Just prior to takeoff he became very excited because they had been on the ground over an hour so Mucklow relayed his displeasure to the cockpit and they answered 'that they had only 1500 pounds of fuel left to be put in, and this was about one-quarter of the total capacity'. Mucklow relayed that to the hijacker and he calmed down.

She then told him it would be a few minutes longer while they filed a flight plan and he replied: "Never mind. They can do that over the radio once we get up.[60] **Let's get the show on the road!"**

The cockpit called to address the issue of Mucklow lowering the stairs once the aircraft was airborne; they told her to use the 'escape rope' to secure herself. Mucklow related this to the hijacker and he vetoed the idea saying "No". He said he didn't want her to go back up front or them to come to the back. Mucklow asked if the Second Officer could shut the front door and he said "Yes". Mucklow got up and opened the rear door and locked it open (as per hijacker's request) and the pilot started the engines and a short time later began taxing toward the runway. During the taxi Mucklow said, **"You know we have oxygen´and the hijacker replied, "Yes I know where it is. If I need it I will get it."**

Mucklow asked him to cut some nylon cord from the parachute for her to use as a safety line when opening the rear ladder (with the door open) and the hijacker said: "Never mind" that he would (open it himself). She showed him where the

---

[59]This is incorrect, the cockpit could not lower the stairs.

[60]This is an interesting tidbit, most non-pilots wouldn't know you could do this.

control panel was and the controls and how to do it, and she reminded him to put the ladder up before landing or the aircraft would be damaged and could not take off again.

She returned to seat 18C, he to 18E, the money was in 18D, and the bomb was in 18F.

The plane took off (with the rear door ajar) and she held her ears because of the loud noise from the engines. Approximately four minutes after take off he stood up and told her to go the cockpit and close the first class curtain, and for no one to come back behind the curtain. The lights were out in the rear compartment and she went forward, faced the curtain, and the last time she saw him he had a nylon cord tied around his waste and he was standing in the aisle. Before she secured the curtain she called back and pleaded with him to take the bomb with him or disarm it before he left.

After securing the curtain she entered the cockpit and approximately ten minutes later, one of the officers received an interphone call from the hijacker advising that he could not get the rear stairs down. The pilot responded that he would 'level the aircraft and reduce the air speed. And a short time later the red indicator light went on on the second officer's panel indicating that the stairs had been lowered, and approximately five minutes after the first call one of the officer's received another call from the hijacker, which was the last communication anyone had with the hijacker.

Before descending at Reno, Mucklow called repeatedly over the intercom system to the hijacker to cooperate, that the aircraft must land. The last message was: "Sir, we are going to land now, please put up the stairs. We are going to land anyway, but the aircraft may be structurally damaged and we may not be able to to take off again after we've landed".

The pilot landed the aircraft and parked it away from the terminal. Mucklow and the pilot entered the cabin area and called to the hijacker a number of times to cooperate, and we asked for instructions (from him). There was no answer so we went behind the curtain. Mucklow went to the galley but did not see the man, and at the same time we flipped on all of the cabin lights and there was no one there.[61]

The Captain and Mucklow ran to the rear of the aircraft and looked for the bomb. Mucklow looked in the aft lavatory and checked the oxygen bottles compartment, then they began crawling up the aisle looking under seats for the bomb. While she was doing this the first officer was coming down the aisle from the cockpit on his knees with a flashlight looking under seats for the bomb. Then after a few more minutes the first officer told her to get off the airplane which she did. Mucklow walked between two blue lights down the taxiway away from the aircraft. It was dark.

Mucklow recalls that upon entering the aft section of the aircraft she saw the one chute that had been cut open and another chute. One was on Row-17, the other on Row-18, both on the left side of the ship.

Mucklow said that about five minutes after she left the aircraft three cars came to the nose of the plane.

Mucklow described the hijacker as follows:
Sex, male. Race, white. Age 44-46. Height 6'. Weight 180-190 lbs. Complexion Medium to dark. Build medium. Hair Dark, flat, straight, sideburns narrow, mid ear. Eyes not observed.
Characteristics: Wore sunglasses, dark plastic wrap around frames.

The man impressed her as being an executive type by his dress, special mannerisms, and consideration that he exhibited for her while he was on the aircraft.

The only time she can recall any actual threat to her life was during the flight from Portland to mention to her to impress on everybody that he

---

[61]FBI agents at Reno claim they entered and cleared the aircraft, finding the crew in a locked cockpit. However, all of the crew reported Scott leaving the cockpit as Mucklow reports here. It's possible both accounts are correct, Capt. Scott and Tina may have left the cockpit to check in on the hijacker, then returned to the cockpit to await the FBI.

would use the device he had, that he would not be taken off the plane. Mucklow could not detect any accent in his voice.

Clothing: Dark brown suit possibly with thin black stripes, brown socks, brown ankle length **pebble grain shoes, not type shoes (loafers).**[62]

She does not recall any rings or facial scars, marks, or tattoos.

Weather: Mucklow advised that her recollection of the flight from Seattle (south) was that the weather was extremely murky and that the ground could not be seen.

---

[62]Much has been made of the fact Cooper is reported to have worn loafers, but Mucklow is the only person to report this, and only here, in her second interview done a week after the first interviews (and the hijacking).

Interview Rataczak 11/24:

William Rataczak was interviewed at the Reno Airport, Reno, Nevada, on the late evening of November 24th and early morning hours of November 25th 1971. He advised he was the Second Officer and Co-pilot on Northwest Airlines Flight #305. Rataczak noted that **he was present during the interviews of Hostess Mucklow and and Third Officer Harold Anderson and concurred with the testimony supplied by them.**[63]

Rataczak recalls the hijacker indicated **the bomb had an 'electrical fuse' and instructed the hostess that radio transmissions be limited as much as possible so that they would not set off the bomb.**

He advised that the landing at Seattle was made at 5:45pm PST, and that the hijacker had indicated that once the money and parachutes were brought on board and refueling was in progress, the passengers would be permitted to leave.

Rataczak stated there was a delay in acquiring the chest type parachutes and when they did not arrive as quickly as hoped for, the crew had Mucklow request permission to land anyway and the hijacker refused.[64] At some point in negotiations the hijacker expressed the belief that the parachutes would be obtained from McChord AFB and indicated that McChord was only 20 miles away from the Seattle Airport.

Rataczak added that after take off at 7:36 pm they received a call from the hijacker at around 7:42pm indicating that he could not get the stairs lowered in flight. We slowed the aircraft down and subsequently the cockpit light indicating the rear stairs were down. At that time the Captain instructed the hijacker to sound the bell on the intercom in the event he wished to make any further contact with them, and he agreed to do so.

---

[63]This is an interesting detail, normally police separate witnesses.

[64]This is contradicted by the notes kept by Flo Schaffner in the cockpit. On the 15th page of notes she writes "If the case waiting for one chest chute, go ahead and go down."

Rataczak added that at no time did he have any direct contact with or observe the hijacker, so could furnish no physical description.

Original Hijacking Notes

These notes were taken by Florence Schaffner during the hijacking and were released by the FBI.

Crew Notes Page #1

Page One[65] of the crew notes gives us a quick review of early details of the hijacking.

---

[65] Nov 24/71 Flight #305 // From Portland--Seattle // Man with briefcase with // a bomb--request $200,000 by 1700 // As I sat down the // stewardess seat. Handed me // a note // and wrote down his request. // 2340--Tina he // doesn't want to wait -- brought // money as far as the stairs // One more request he // wants the notes back // he will let everybody // off as soon as // he get his request // & a fuel

> note oops:
>
> miss —
> I have a bomb in
> my briefcase + want
> you to sit by me.
> He told me to
> write it in a
> piece of paper upon
> his request
>
> (upside down)
> He requested
> Tina
> Like money first
> then passengers can go.

Crew Notes Page #2

The second page[66] gives us what is likely to be the exact wording of the original note Cooper gave Florence Schaffner.

---

[66]Note says: // Miss-- // I have a bomb in // my briefcase & want // you to sit by me. // He tells me to // write it in a // piece of paper upon// his request // (upside down) He requested // Tina // Like money first // then passengers can go.

Crew Notes Pages #3 & #4

Page three[67] gives a quick description of the hijacker from Flo while page four[68] gives a timeline of the early hijacking.

---

[67]He's got black hair // wearing dark raincoat. // He is in his 50's // Around 175 lbs. // 6'1" // Seating--row 18 in // the middle seat very // back of the aircraft.

[68]2259-- T. Called Phone // being hijacked // no joke. // 2202--Flo in cockpit with // note // 2305 -- 2nd call from // Tina concerning // mat[ter]. has bomb // with a // 2310 -- wants money in // negotiable currency // to be passed [to a] // crew member. // 2320 -- wants everything // ready before // landing

Crew Notes Pages #5 & #6

Page five[69] is interesting since it appears Tina didn't want to be stuck babysitting the hijacker. Page six[70] includes Cooper's paranoia about sky marshals plus a promise from the hijacker to disconnect the bomb if things went right.

---

[69] 2325 -- wants to hold out // without passengers // knowing if possible // 23262 -- people can leave // A/C after complete fueling. // 23302 -- Holding NW Sea // 6000 18,00 (?) fuel remaining // 2343 -- call from company // standing by // 2345 -- sit rep to [MPLS? map?] // ops. // Tina called would like // let the other girl stay // back with him he said // no.

[70] Tina // his first concern was // people going back of the // aircraft--he think its // sky marshall. // 0600(?) -- PA to passengers // telling them we have // mechanical trouble // he will reassure not // trying anything -- did //not want to scare (her) // if their was attempt // he will disonnect the // bomb. // He requested fuel truck // $200,000 2 chest packs

Crew Notes Pages #7 & #8

We get our first set of instructions on how Cooper wants the money to be brought on board on page seven.[71] Page eight[72] includes more instructions from Cooper.

---

[71] Tine -- Bill talking -- // telling her the // money secured // available for him // by 5 // He wants tina to // go down stairs and // get the money -- people // seated until Tina // return. Have a // Truck (w?) stairs. // extra car--with money. // Money brought it by // truck-- He doesn't care // when money trucks // get there--all he cares

[72] 1) money first // 2) passenger off // 3) then chutes // 4) fueling commence // upon landing // On (??) 18 min. // (??) // Capt. Bill // Co-pilot--Bill Raticheck // 2nd officer.

Crew Notes Pages #9 & #10

Page nine[73] is a mess, it includes a description of the bomb and we get more indications that Cooper wasn't enjoying how long everything was taking. Page ten[74] is interesting, apparently Cooper thought the chutes would be coming from McChord AFB.

---

[73] (Tina called) He said // [?areas w??ed all fine?] // Fine -- Redstick // large battery and // a wire // hijacker // getting anxious -- // Looking two chest types chutes -- 10min // everything at airport // nobodycomesback row 15 // Flo sat in fr. seat // of T.C/ section-- // re???e-- // people to sit down until they are told (hustle?) // (always?) to (??let) seated // Tell him to sit down // until Capt to advice them to // get from their seat

[74] Tina--wants to know // ("Hijacker") why climbing -- // --still waiting-- // for 2 parachutes // money & gas on the // way // "He" said why it took // money & chutes longtime. // --Chutee came from-- // McCrd airforce base. // He does wants to // wait for the chutes // before we land. // 5 to 10 min.

Crew Notes Pages #11 & #12

Cooper expresses more concern with how long it was taking to get the parachutes.[75] "Al" mentioned in page twelve[76] is Al Lee, operations manager for Northwest Orient in Seattle. He delivered the money to the plane wearing a trench coat over his pilot uniform to avoid Cooper mistaking him for law enforcement.

---

[75]Hurry up the chutes // Hijacker advice Tina. // getting very impatient // of the chutes. // 2 bag packs // Have money // money first // Tina--asking again // heard of a chute // one suggestion allowed to land // He doesn't want to wait // at all. In order to // fuel aircraft 10 to 20

[76]no funny stuffs happening // Name-- // as soon // Tina called // as we completely // stop--refueling as// soon as possible. // Al -- tan trench coat // on // PDX--man prescription // P.A. -- 0045 advising // was not genuine // mechanincal problem // existant that reassured // passenger fuel burn off will // [?ready?] landing 13 to 18 min.

> no action
> Tina – ~~pos~~ no body in the aisle
>
> money at control go out in field with money —
>
> Tina — people stay on board while the plane is being fueled — after being fuel — people can get off —
> Tina get the money.

Crew Notes Page # 13

Page thirteen clarifies (again) how Cooper wants the money brought on board.[77]

---

[77] no action // Tina--nobody in // the aisle // money at control // go out in field // with money -- // Tina--people stay on //board while the // plane is being // fueled--after // being fuel--people // can get off--- // Tina get the // money

Crew Notes Page #14

It's unclear whether it's Bill Rataczak deciding where to put the aircraft, or if these were instructions from Cooper[78]

---

[78]Bill - make approach // advise him going // to airport // money--available // chutes available // want to keep the // aircraft from the ramp & find an // area that is lighted // Area partially lighted. // 1) making approach 2) request available. Hijacker says fine.

Crew Notes Page #15

Cooper, apparently sick of waiting on the Chest chutes, relents and is willing to land without them being ready.[79]

---

[79] If the case waiting // for one chest chute go // ahead & go down

Acknowledgements

This has been a long journey for me; I have spent the last two years trapped down the deep rabbit hole that is the Cooper hijacking. It's easy to get lost in such a place, so I need to thank my manuscript reviewers who helped me navigate the world outside the cave. In particular, I want to thank my editors Bill Gilles, Marty Wingard, and Aaron Clarey. Bill had some fantastic ideas on how to increase the literary value of this book, most of which I ended up ignoring. If you felt lost in the details of this case, or confused at any point, it would have been much worse without Bill. Marty deserves special recognition for his line-editing. For years I only read books by dead authors which gave me an archaic understanding of English prose. Marty punched up the narrative and made my arguments more direct and succinct. An impossible task, but one he took on cheerfully. Then there's Aaron... If you need help with some aspect of your life, whether financial or financial, or personal, but mostly financial, I would recommend Aaron Clarey's company Asshole Consulting at assholeconsulting.com.

Another huge thanks goes out to my father, Martin Andrade Sr., for helping me understand the basics of aviation navigation, parachuting, the 727, airline procedures, and the SAGE radar system, plus pretty much everything else related to the Norjak case. He also edited and reviewed the entire book, adding his own insights to the final product. His contributions were especially important in understanding the flight path of 305. Humorously, he corrected many of Mr. Wingard's corrections, suggesting he was "fighting the dead prose of the modern world," or something like that.

Special acknowledgment needs to go to all the guys at the various Cooper forums, they include but are not limited to Dave Brown (AKA Shutter), Bruce Smith, Farflung, SafecrackingPLF, eVicki (daughter of Mel Wilson), 377, Robert Nicholson (AKA Robert99), Georger, Mark Bennett, Ross Richardson (AKA nmiwrecks), Snowmman, Sluggo, and a few dozen others. The collective research done by all these people made this book possible. Few, if any, of these online sleuths will agree with my conclusions. In fact, I'll probably be ridiculed on the forums relentlessly until the sun becomes a red giant and consumes the Earth. I look forward to it.

Thanks to Ben Wetmore for coming up with a decent cover for the first Kindle Edition.

Though I never interacted with him, this book would not have been possible without the research done by Tom Kaye, Carol Abraczinskas and the rest of the Citizen Sleuths team. They did the heavy lifting when it came to the particles on Cooper's tie, understanding the Tena Bar money find, and confirming 305's true flight path. FBI Special Agent Larry Carr deserves praise for his willingness to open up the case to the public, which reinvigorated interest in Norjak and led to a renaissance in the case. Finally, I should thank Jo Weber, former wife of Duane Weber. Jo had extensive contact with Max Gunther and helped me understand some details about his book and his contact with Clara. Near the end of his life, Max Gunther was still trying to find the true identity of "Clara" and "Dan LeClair" and it appears Jo's forceful belief that Duane was D.B. Cooper had convinced him he had the true story. I don't believe Duane was Cooper, but the fact Gunther was so interested in Jo's story is another piece of evidence against the the idea that Gunther's book was a hoax.

As always, anything a value found herein is because these wonderful people mentioned above; any weaknesses are mine alone.

About the Authors

Martin Andrade Jr. is a writer, novelist and author who recently penned "Richard Nixon's Guide to the Multiverse", a novel about all the things he finds ridiculous about existence. His blog, which is somehow still a thing, is located on the internet at martinandrade.wordpress.com. A graduate of the University of Minnesota, he has been searching for the perfect burger since 2005.

Martin Andrade Sr. is a graduate of the Air Force Academy and spent more than twenty years serving his country in the United States Air Force, including several hundred combat sorties over Vietnam. He received parachute training at the U.S. Army Airborne school at Fort Benning. After the Air Force, he spent the next fifteen years of his life flying large jets for United Airlines, retiring in 2004. He currently spends his time reading, exercising, and forcing the world's laziest dog to go on long walks.

FBI Sketches of DB Cooper (From FBI Archives)

Made in United States
Troutdale, OR
03/14/2025